Childcraft
The How and Why Library

Volume 8

How We Get Things

Field Enterprises Educational Corporation

Chicago Frankfurt London Paris Rome Sydney Tokyo Toronto

A subsidiary of
Field Enterprises, Inc. fe

Acknowledgments

The publishers of *Childcraft—The How and Why Library*
gratefully acknowledge the courtesy of the following
publishers, agencies, and corporations for permission
to use copyrighted illustrations. Full illustration
acknowledgments for this volume appear on pages
378–379.

Page 24: Photography by Arthur Rickerby, *Life*
© Time Inc.

Page 139 (bottom): Photography by George Burns,
The Saturday Evening Post, © Curtis Publishing Co.

Pages 286–287 (top): Photography by Dmitri Kessel,
Life, © Time Inc.

Volume 8

How We Get Things

Contents

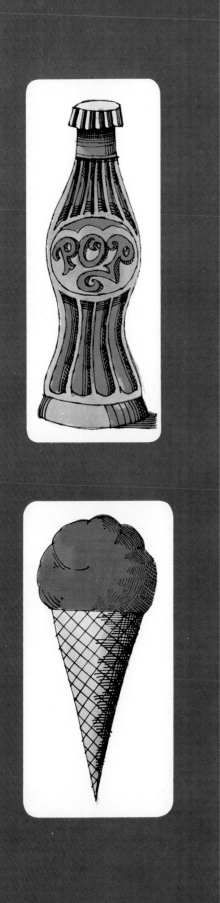

Meals
and Treats

How does ice cream get its flavor?
When is a sausage a block long?
Why does gelatin shiver?
Why does pop fizz?
Where is the corn in cornflakes?
How does the chew get
in chewing gum?
Where does Swiss cheese get
its holes?

Read on and you will see.

Ice-cream flavors

People who make ice cream mix cream and milk together with sugar and gelatin. The mixture is then frozen.

To make plain ice cream, they add ground-up pods from an orchid plant that grows in Mexico and Madagascar. The plant is called vanilla.

To make chocolate ice cream, they add the ground-up beans from the cacao tree that grows in Central and South America.

6

To make green pistachio ice cream, they add the ground-up kernel of the pistachio nut that grows on trees in Europe and Asia.

To make fruit ice cream, they add strawberries from a strawberry plant, or cherries from a cherry tree, or bananas from a banana plant.

Ice-cream machines

The flavor is in the flavor funnels.
The ingredients are in the storage tanks.
The operator is stationed at the control panel.
Everything is ready.

Now the operator pushes the start button.
Begin Operation Ice Cream.

In large ice-cream plants, special machinery
can make about 2,000 gallons (7,600 liters)
of ice cream every hour.
And one man who sits at a control panel
can start the machinery going by pushing
a start button.

He pushes other buttons
and turns dials attached to tanks,
which contain sugar, syrup, flavoring,
and other stuff that make ice cream.
The tanks then pump
just the right amount
of each ingredient into a huge vat.
The vat shakes and mixes
all the ingredients.
Then the mixture
goes into a freezer where it thickens.

More machines put the mixture into containers
and send it to a freezing tunnel.
End Operation Ice Cream.

Back to the control panel.
Now the operator pushes more buttons on the panel
and all the machines in the plant
are washed and steamed and sterilized for use the next day.

Animal crackers

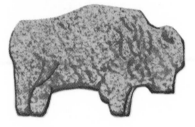

There is a bear snoozing near my spoon,
and an elephant is about to trumpet in his ear.
A giraffe is peeking out of a box at me,
and a hippopotamus is leaning on my fork.
These are not real animals—
they are animal crackers
that are cut from cooky dough at a bakery.

The animal cutouts are baked
until they are crisp and crunchy.
Then, lions and tigers
are wrapped with elephants, bears, and hippopotamuses
and put in a box.

The only chance I get to pinch the nose of a bear,
nibble an elephant's trunk,
swallow a giraffe's neck,
or push a whole hippopotamus in my mouth
is when I eat animal crackers.

weighing cookies

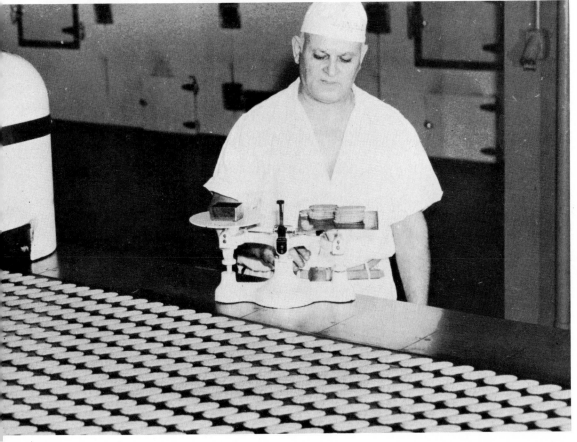

Taffy apples

A stick is good for
fishing or
for roasting marshmallows,
or for holding a taffy apple.

To make a taffy apple, you
push a stick into an apple
and then dip the apple
into a kettle of sticky caramel.
But before the caramel gets hard,
you roll the apple
in a pan of crushed nuts.
Now the taffy apple
is ready for you to eat.

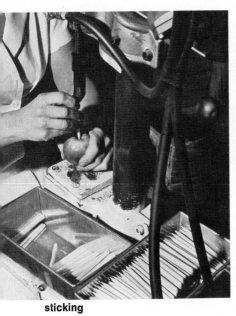

sticking

dipping

rolling

packing

What's the fizz?

The fizz you see floating to the top of a bottle of pop is a bubbly gas. But when the bubbles pop at the top, you can't see the gas anymore. The gas has no color. It is almost like air.

At the bottling factory, the gas is pumped into flavored water—orange, grape, strawberry, or any other flavor you want.

You can put the cap back on a bottle of pop. But you can't put the fizz back in the pop!

PAUL McNEAR

plumping

drying

powdering

Skin and bones

What food is made from the skins and bones of animals? Gelatin!

The skins and bones are cleaned. Then both are put in a tank of acid. The skins and bones (called stock) are stirred very fast for several hours. This process "plumps" the skins.

After plumping, the stock is heated several times. Gelatin is removed after each heating. The gelatin is filtered, dried, cooled, and spread in layers to set. The layers of gelatin are next cut into sheets and moved to drying nets. Finally, it is ground into a powder and packaged.

When your mother makes gelatin dessert that tastes like lemon, raspberry, grape, or orange, she uses gelatin that has been mixed with sugar, fruit flavoring, and other things. She pours hot water into the powder and stirs it. Then she puts it into the refrigerator to harden—not as hard as bone—just solid enough so that it wiggles and shakes when you poke your spoon into it.

A few puffs of smoke quiet the bees.

A honey extractor removes the honey from the honeycombs.

Food from honeybees

Who put the honey in the jar?
It wasn't your mother
or the grocery man.
It was a honey-pouring machine
that uses honey from honeycombs.

Who got the honey
out of the honeycombs?
It wasn't a honey bear
or a honey badger.
It was a machine
called a honey extractor.
The honey extractor
whirls the honeycombs
around and around
until the honey flows out.

And who put the honey in the combs?
It wasn't a bumblebee
or a wasp.
It was the honeybee!

Swiss cheese holes

What makes the holes in Swiss cheese?
They are made by bacteria.
These are not the kind of bacteria
that make you sick,
but these are *safe* bacteria.

In cheese factories, the bacteria
are mixed with milk in huge vats.
The bacteria make the solid part
of the milk, or curd,
separate from the liquid part
of the milk, or whey.

Soon the milk begins to ripen or ferment.
As it ferments,
the bacteria make air bubbles.
And the air bubbles
are the holes in Swiss cheese.

mixing

pressing

storing

ready to eat

Bread is light and airy because of tiny plants
called yeasts that are mixed into the dough.

Why bread puffs up

Bread puffs up like a balloon before it is baked. Tiny plants that are mixed in the dough make the bread puff up. The tiny plants are called yeasts. They don't look like the green, leafy plants you see in lawns and gardens. They look like drops of clear jelly! And they are so small they can be seen only with a microscope.

Yeast plants use sugar as food. So bakers mix yeast and sugar together in bread dough. When the yeast plants take in sugar, they change part of it to a gas. The gas makes many tiny bubbles swell up in the dough. This makes the dough puff up like a balloon. When the puffed-up dough is baked, it becomes a loaf of light, airy bread.

Stuffing sausage skins

It would take three buckets of mustard, a barrel of relish, and a field of onions to cover a hot dog that is a block long. And that is how long a hot dog is when it is first made.

Sausage makers pour ground-up meat into a sausage-stuffing machine. The meat squirts from a nozzle into a folded sausage skin. As the skin is stuffed, it unfolds and wriggles and slides from side to side. It gets longer and longer.

Soon the stuffed sausage skin is nearly a block long. But it would be hard to eat a hot dog that is so long! So another machine pinches and nips the long sausage into a string of hot dogs, small enough to fit in a bun.

Stiff, skinny spaghetti

Spaghetti looks as stiff and skinny as broom straws when you take it from the package. But before it got into the package, it looked like cooked spaghetti, soft enough to twirl around your fork.

At spaghetti factories, workers use many machines. One machine mixes a special flour with some boiling water. The mixture goes into another machine that pounds it into dough. Still another machine presses the dough through small holes that shape it into soft spaghetti.

Next, the soft spaghetti is cut into lengths to fit the spaghetti package. The soft spaghetti dries until stiff in a heated room.

After inspectors check the dried spaghetti, machines sort it, weigh it, and pack it. Then it is ready to be made soft again, when your mother cooks it.

Macaroni is made from the same kind of dough as spaghetti, but it is a little thicker and has a hole through it like a drinking straw.

A machine makes strings of spaghetti.

Where is the corn in cornflakes?

It is easy to see corn kernels when they are on the cob or before they pop into popcorn. But what happens to the corn kernels that turn into cornflakes?

First, they are shelled from the cob and soaked in a special liquid that removes the skins and other parts. What's left of a kernel is called a corn grit. The grits are flavored, cooked, and dried. Then, a machine flattens the grits into flakes that are toasted until they crinkle into crunchy cornflakes.

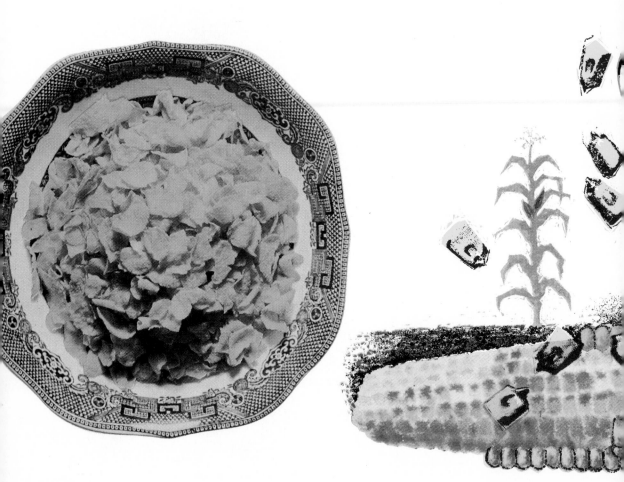

A high-speed oven toasts
raw cornflakes.

How does a doughnut get a hole?

The hole in a doughnut can be something to eat around, or stick a finger in, or peek through. But you cannot eat it, and you cannot hold it. And once you eat the doughnut, the hole is gone.

A machine puts the hole in a doughnut. It punches the doughnut out of a flat piece of dough, the way your mother cuts out cookies with a cooky cutter. Then the doughnut, hole and all, is put in boiling oil. The oil bubbles through the hole and around the doughnut until it is puffy and crisp. Without a hole, a doughnut just wouldn't be a doughnut. It would be a fried cake.

In a large bakery, a long belt moves
the doughnuts from hole-punching to frying.

31

Chewing chicle

What puts the chew in chewing gum?
It's chicle!
Chicle is a rubbery juice
that oozes out of a tree called a sapodilla tree.

At a gum factory, chicle is mixed in large kettles
with sugar and corn syrup.
Some flavoring, like spearmint or peppermint, is added.

Then a machine rolls the gum into thin sheets,
larger than a newspaper page,
and marks out the sticks.
Another machine, called a gum breaker, breaks
the marked sheets into sticks.
Still another machine wraps and packs the sticks
into packages of gum.

Bubble gum is made like all other chewing gum.
But a little rubber is mixed with the chicle
to make the bubble gum strong enough
for you to blow bubbles that don't break easily.

marking sticks

wrapping

Fields of food

Some foods are grown in fields. Usually, they cannot be eaten right away. First, they must be harvested or gathered. Then, the crops are sent to factories to be made into food.

Sugar cane grows where it is hot. The tall stalks are harvested by workers or machines. A worker uses a machete, a big, flat-bladed knife, to cut the cane. After it is cut down, the sugar cane is sent to a factory where it is made into sugar.

Farmers harvest their crops, also. Cutting machines called combines cut the wheat, oats, and barley quickly. Wheat and oats are used to make flour. Most of our baked goods are made from these grains. Barley is used to flavor food and feed cattle.

combine

Sweet, sticky syrup

Drippy, sticky maple syrup tastes good on pancakes, French toast, and even ice cream.

Where does maple syrup come from? It comes from trees— black maples and sugar maples.

Is it hard to get syrup from a tree? No, it's easy from early March to late April. First, a hole is drilled in the tree. Then, a metal or wooden spout is stuck into the hole. A bucket or plastic bag is hung on the spout. The sap drips, drips, drips from the tree, down the spout, and into the bag or bucket.

Next, trucks or horse-drawn sleighs take workers from tree to tree to gather the sap. The bags or buckets are emptied into large tanks. The sap is hauled to the sugarhouse. Here, it is boiled for several hours until it becomes syrup.

To make sure the syrup tastes good, the workers and their children often hold sugaring off parties. They take fresh, hot syrup and pour it on a mound of snow. Using spoons, everyone digs into their homemade, syrup-and-snow sundae.

37

Turning potatoes into potato chips

Potato chips are pieces of potato cut nearly as thin as paper. People who make the chips use a tool called a micrometer to make sure the slices are not too thick or too thin.

The thin slices of raw potato are put into big pots of boiling oil. The slices sizzle and sputter and curl up in the boiling oil until they become crunchy, curly potato chips.

Seafood

Clams and cod, shrimp and sardines, haddock and herring—these are all foods we get from the sea. We bake, fry, broil, and boil them, and even eat some raw. How do we get seafood from the sea?

Fishermen often catch fish by dragging nets in the ocean. Before the fishermen go out to sea, they mend their nets. This keeps the fish from slipping through big holes in the net.

Some fishermen catch tuna with poles, lines, and hooks. A big tuna fish may take three fishermen to catch it. All three lines from their poles are fastened to one hook.

Trained birds called cormorants catch fish for their owners in the Orient. The birds dive into the water, catch the fish, and bring them to the fishermen's boats. Metal bands around the birds' necks keep them from swallowing the fish.

Fishermen sometimes catch big swordfish by using long spears called harpoons. The fishermen hurl or shoot a harpoon at the fish. A long line with a floating marker is fastened to the harpoon. The marker shows the fishermen where the fish goes after it is hit.

fishermen catching tuna

fishing with cormorants

fishing with a harpoon

41

Milk to you

A dairy farmer uses hoses on milking machines to get milk from his cows. The milk then goes through a pipeline and into a tank that cools it.

A man from a dairy plant uses a pipe to run the milk from the cooling tank into his truck. When he gets back to the dairy plant, he runs the milk through other pipes from his truck to large tanks. These tanks keep the milk cold.

Workers in the dairy plant let the milk flow from the tanks through shiny pipes. The milk goes to machines that make it clean and safe to drink. Still other pipes carry it to a bottling machine and into clean glass bottles and paper cartons.

After the milk is bottled, workers have to clean the pipes in the dairy plant. They take all the pipes down. They soap them, brush them, rinse them, and steam them. Then they put the pipes back, clean and shiny, for the next day's milk.

bottling

A butter-print machine cuts and wraps the butter.

Where does butter come from?

Butter doesn't come from butterflies or buttercups. Butter comes from milk. Milk is full of tiny, round globules of fat, and we use these fat globules to make butter.

In butter factories, the cream from milk is poured into tanks that look like great big drums. The drums turn and churn the cream. As the cream churns, the globules of fat come together to make tiny clumps of butter. The clumps come together to make lumps of butter. The rest of the cream, the part that doesn't clump and lump into butter, is drained from the drum. That's what we call buttermilk. All that is left in the drum, then, are lumps of butter. The lumps are washed in cold water. Some are salted. Then a machine cuts the butter into blocks, wraps it in paper, and puts it into packages.

A dairy truck takes it to the store where your mother buys it. Now it is ready for you to spread on your bread.

Getting food ready

People use knives, saws, and other cutting tools to get food ready for cooking and eating.

A cook uses a paring knife for peeling vegetables and a saw-edged knife for slicing tomatoes. He uses a food chopper for cutting up vegetables and a curved knife for scooping out grapefruits. He has a long, thin knife with tiny teeth that slices soft bread without tearing it. He has a sharp slicing knife for carving meats. Even the can opener he uses is a knife.

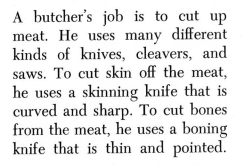

A butcher's job is to cut up meat. He uses many different kinds of knives, cleavers, and saws. To cut skin off the meat, he uses a skinning knife that is curved and sharp. To cut bones from the meat, he uses a boning knife that is thin and pointed.

When a butcher has to cut through bone, he uses a saw or a cleaver. A cleaver is something like a hatchet. When he wants to grind meat for hamburger, a butcher uses a meat grinder. The grinder pushes the meat through a knife that turns. To cut meat into even slices, a butcher uses a machine with a round knife that spins.

Many mouths to feed

A chef is the head cook in a fancy restaurant. A chef uses big pots and pans to cook for his customers. He may make huge pots of soup, large roasts of beef, and big bowls of pudding.

A candymaker makes large amounts of candy at one time. He mixes candy from caramel, chocolate, honey, nuts, eggs, cream, and fruit. Then he pours the different mixtures into pans to cool or to cook.

Bakers bake many loaves of bread at once. They mix flour, yeast, water, and other ingredients together to make the bread dough. After the dough rises in a long pan, it is baked in smaller loaf pans.

candymakers

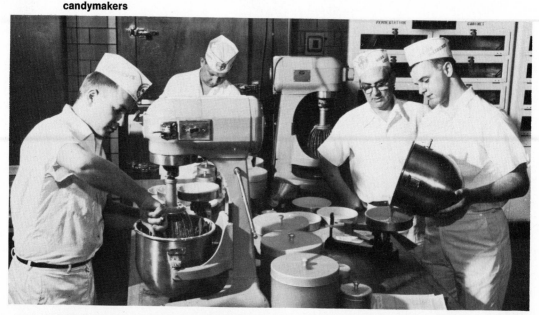

baker

chef

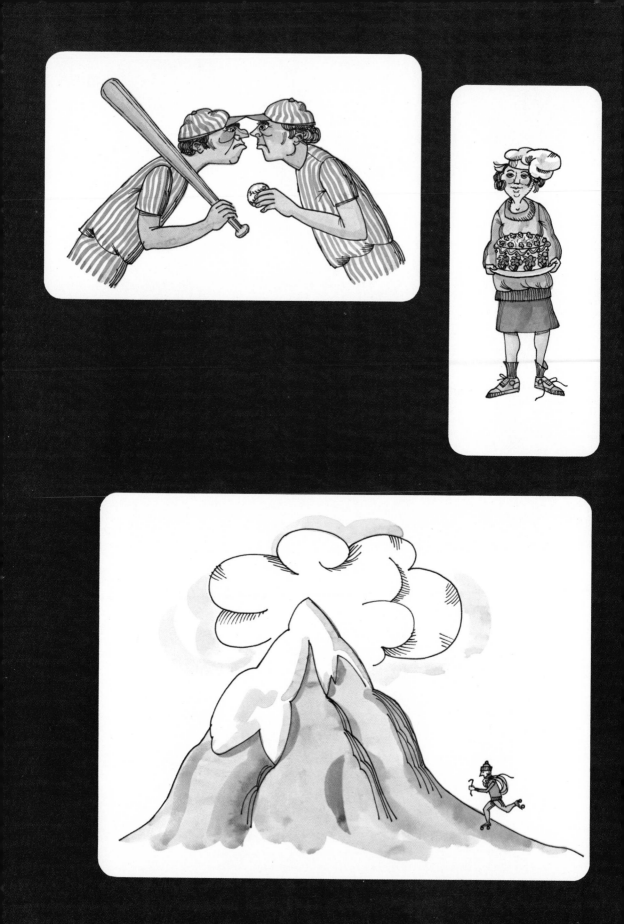

The Things We Wear

If all baseball players wore exactly
the same uniforms,
it would be hard to tell
which team had won.
People often get clothes
that show who they are.

If firemen wore bathing suits
while fighting a fire,
they would probably be burned.
People often wear clothes
that protect them.

If you saw a baker wearing
a sweat shirt,
you might not buy her cookies.
Some people must wear clothes
that look fresh and clean.

If a mountain climber wore
roller skates,
he would not travel very far.
People often get clothes
that help them move about.

Read on and you will learn more
about the things we wear.

51

Hats for workers

Sailors wear one kind of hat.
Cowboys wear another kind.
Judges in England wear wigs.
And kings and queens
sometimes wear crowns.
Some hats and things people
wear on their heads
show what kind of work they do.

Look at these pictures
and see if you can tell
who does what.

Can you find the skycap
who carries suitcases for you
at the airport?

Which is the engineer who drives
the railroad train?

Which one is the railroad conductor
who collects the passengers' tickets?

Can you find the chef
who is cooking a meal?

Which is the professor dressed up
for graduation day?

Which is the nurse
who works in a hospital?

Which one is the English soldier
who wears a hat called a bearskin?

And which one is the bullfighter
waiting to enter the arena?

These people wear special hats
when they do their work.
Many other workers, too,
wear hats or helmets
that help them do their jobs.

Hats that get bumped

Some people work where they might get bumped on the head. So they wear hard hats or helmets to keep from getting hurt.

Men who work on high buildings wear hard safety hats to protect their heads from tools and other things that might fall.

Men who drill oil wells wear safety hats, too.

A racing-car driver zooming around a racetrack wears a crash helmet to protect his head in case he crashes.

A football player wears a padded helmet to protect his head from the bumps he gets in a football game.

When a baseball player in the big leagues goes to bat, he puts on a hard cap. It protects his head from any wild pitches. Little League players wear hard caps, too.

A boxer also wears a head protector. But he wears it only when he is practicing before a fight.

racing-car drivers

football players

baseball players

boxers

Suits that are part of a job

Some people wear suits that are almost a part of their work.
Since long ago, people have worn the same kinds of suits for these jobs.

In Spain, Mexico, and South America a bullfighter wears a suit
that is covered with braids and sparkling beads. He calls it his
suit of lights. His suit is part of the beauty of a bullfighter's
graceful motions. He waves his cape and makes the bull do
exactly what he wants it to do.

A ringmaster in a circus announces every act. "LADIES AND GENTLEMEN!" he calls. Then he tells you what will happen next. But even before he says a word, you know he is the ringmaster. He is carrying a hat that is tall and black. And he is all dressed up in a fancy coat that is short in front and long in back.

In many courts a judge wears a robe that is long and black. When he walks in, another man calls, "Hear ye! Hear ye! The court is now in session." In the court, the judge represents the law. His job is to see that arguments are settled according to the law.

Health masks

In fire and smoke

When a fireman has to go into a burning, smoke-filled building, he often wears a mask.

It helps to keep out choking smoke and gas, so that the fireman can fight the fire.

At the hospital

A doctor sometimes wears a white cloth mask to protect his patients from germs.

A nurse wears the same kind of mask in the nursery to keep germs away from little babies.

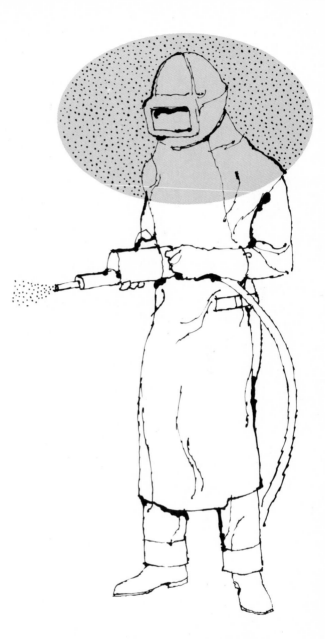

Out on the range

Where the cowboy works, it is often dry and dusty. The cattle stir up clouds of dust. And if there is any wind, the dust gets blown around.

Then the cowboy pulls his kerchief over his mouth and nose. The kerchief keeps the dust out.

On the side of a building

A sandblaster cleans brick and stone buildings with a hose that shoots sand.

His big round mask keeps the sand out of his nose, and mouth, and eyes, and ears.

Masks that protect

When sparks fly

A man who joins pieces of metal together is called a welder. He may use an electric torch, which shoots sparks, or a blowtorch with a hot, bright flame.

A welder wears a mask to protect his face from sparks and bright light. His mask has a small window in it made of dark glass. This window allows the welder to see without danger to his eyes.

The ladle man at the steel mill

A steelworker who pours hot steel into molds must protect his eyes, too. The hot steel gives off a blinding, bright light. The steelworker wears goggles made of heavy, dark glass.

Out at the ballpark

During a baseball game there is one player, the catcher, who always wears a mask to protect his face. The umpire who stands behind the catcher also wears a mask.

In front of the catcher and the umpire is the batter who faces the pitcher. When the pitcher throws the ball, the batter tries to hit it. Very often, the ball flies backward off his bat. When it does, it may smash against the catcher's or umpire's mask.

This mask has bars. The bars are like bumpers on a car. The catcher and the umpire can see between the bars that keep the ball from hitting their faces.

Suits to wear underwater

Frogmen have to swim fast and far underwater. In wartime, one of their jobs is to find enemy bombs in the water and fix them so they won't blow up.

When frogmen have to swim through cold water, they keep warm by wearing long suits made of rubber. The suits fit tightly so the frogmen can swim fast and glide easily through the water.

A deep-sea diver wears a diving suit
when he goes deep underwater.
The deeper he goes, the harder the water
presses against his suit.

If he went too deep without his diving suit,
the water would press against him so hard
that it might crush him.

His suit is fastened to his helmet.
His helmet is fastened to a hose.
The hose is fastened to a machine.
The machine is above the water.
It pumps air through the hose,
into his helmet, and into his diving suit.

The air puffs up the suit.
The suit presses back against the water.
And it keeps the deep-sea diver
from getting crushed.

Circus shoes

A clown's job is to make people laugh.
One way that he does this is to waddle
around on long, flat, floppy shoes.
He can use his shoes to be even funnier.

He stops and leans—and leans—and leans
until you think he'll fall over.
What's the secret of his floppy shoes?

On the bottom of his shoes are some metal clips.
They fit into other metal clips fastened to the floor.
When the clown stands in the right place, he can lean
forward or backward or over to the side.
The clips on his shoes and on the floor keep him
from falling.

The tightrope walker and his shoes

The circus tightrope walker's job is
to walk on nothing but a wire
high in the air.

When he takes a step, he sways.
He moves his arms. He leans.
He shifts his weight from side to side.
He bends his feet and toes.
And he keeps his balance on the wire.

To help him keep his balance, he
wears soft leather shoes. His soft
leather soles let him feel the wire with
his feet. They help him make sure
his feet are in place every time he
takes a step.

Suits that make us laugh

You may think that a clown is a clown,
but there are many different kinds of clowns.
Two basic kinds are the whiteface and the auguste.

The whiteface clown paints his face white,
and colors his nose and mouth.
His baggy costume has big ruffles
and he always wears a cone-shaped hat.
There is something about him that is both gentle and sad.

The auguste also paints his face white,
but he paints on more color than the whiteface does.
His clown costume may make him look like a tired tramp,
a funny fireman, or a pudgy policeman.
He often wears a colorful, long-haired wig.

Children love the auguste because he bothers the whiteface
and makes a mess of everything.
He may be chased by a dog or get splashed with water.

No two circus clowns look exactly the same.
Each has his own funny makeup and special costume.

67

Suits for going up

An astronaut has to wear a space suit whenever he leaves his spacecraft to take a walk in outer space or on the surface of the moon.

There is no air in outer space. Without air, there is no oxygen to breathe. Air also presses against us, and too much or too little air pressure can hurt us.

An astronaut's space suit has machines that give him the oxygen he needs. These machines pump oxygen for him to breathe and also surround his body with the right amount of air pressure.

With his protective space suit on, an astronaut can open the hatch of his spacecraft and go for a walk in safety in space or on the moon.

An Apollo 15 astronaut was protected by his space suit while he walked on the moon.

The daring young man on the flying trapeze
flies through the air with the greatest of ease.

He wears a suit that fits him tightly.
There are no ruffles or frills on it.
There is nothing to get in his way.

Back and forth, he swings and swoops,
faster and farther with every swing.
When he swings out as far as he can,
he lets go and leaps to catch another trapeze.
He can do daring somersaults in the air,
and you hold your breath until—
another trapeze artist catches him.

Suits that keep you from getting burned

Sometimes the firemen at an airport have to walk right through a fire to rescue people.

To do it, they wear flameproof rescue suits that cover them from head to toe.

The rescue suits are as shiny as the wrapper on a stick of gum. They are coated with aluminum.

Heat from the flames bounces off the aluminum, and the firemen don't get burned.

Many steel-mill workers work where it is hot.
Some run machines that dump steel into blazing
furnaces. Some stand near giant ladles that pour
hot melted iron. Some take samples of boiling
steel from the furnaces. And when the steel is
ready, other workers open the furnaces to let the
white-hot steel gush out like a river of fire.

To keep from getting burned, these steel-mill
workers wear flameproof clothes coated with
shiny aluminum. Heat from the hot iron and
steel bounces off the shiny clothes and away
from the workers.

White suits
and aprons

Many doctors and nurses
and dentists and barbers
wear white clothes while they work.
They are guarding your health
or making you look good.
They have to look clean.

Many butchers and bakers
and sausage makers
and chefs and dairy workers
and the people who make ice cream
wear white clothes when they work, too.
They are fixing the food that you eat.
They have to keep clean.

White is a good color to wear when
you have to look clean in your work.

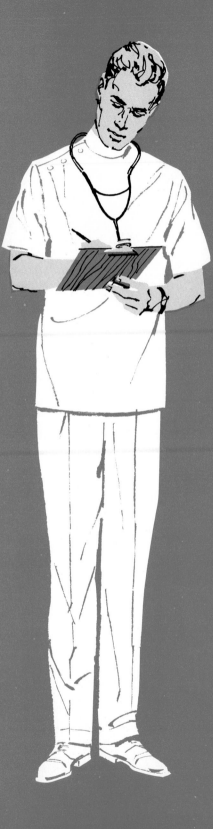

Suits with pads or chaps

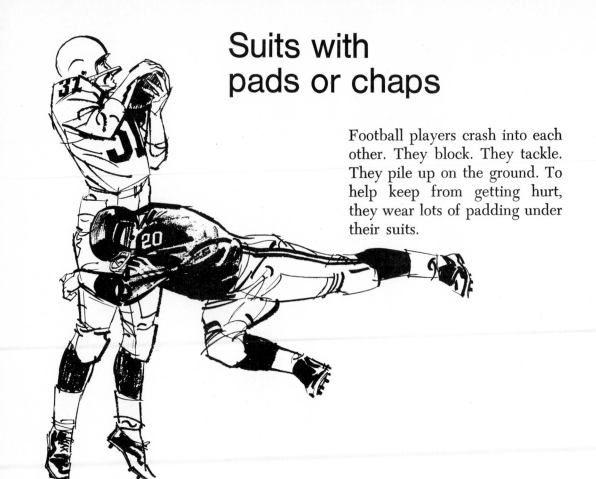

Football players crash into each other. They block. They tackle. They pile up on the ground. To help keep from getting hurt, they wear lots of padding under their suits.

Ice-hockey players also wear padding to keep from getting hurt when they slam into each other, or get hit with the puck, or a hockey stick, or the blades of a player's skates. The goalie on the team wears the most padding of all.

Sometimes the catcher in a baseball game gets hit with a ball or a bat. That's why he wears shin guards and a chest protector. The umpire who stands behind the catcher also wears a chest protector.

batwing chaps

shotgun chaps   angora chaps

A cowboy wears extra protection, too. He wears leather chaps over his blue jeans. His chaps protect his legs when he rides through sagebrush and cactus. They protect his legs when he's riding an ornery horse that tries to bite him or rub him against a fence. They protect him when he ropes a horse and holds the rope tight across his legs.

Suits that show who's who

A Landing Signal Officer or LSO helps a pilot land his plane on the deck of an aircraft carrier.

Usually, the LSO gives directions to the pilot by radio, while the pilot watches a lighted mirror on the flight deck.

But when a rough sea rocks the carrier so badly that the pilot cannot use the mirror, the LSO, dressed in an orange suit, waves brightly colored paddles to help the pilot land safely.

Referees make sure basketball and football games are played according to the rules. When a player breaks a rule, a referee signals to the scorekeepers to tell them what happened. The scorekeepers know who to watch because referees wear shirts with black and white stripes.

Uniforms with bright colors and big numbers show which skater belongs to what team in Roller Derby. This sport is fast and rough. Players score points by gaining a lap on skaters of the other team and then passing them.

When jockeys ride horses in a race, they wear shiny suits called "silks." Their trousers are white, but their shirts and hats have flashy colors. No two jockeys wear the same colors. THEY'RE OFF! The horses thunder down the track. How can you tell which horse is which? Look at the colors of the jockeys' shirts.

Suits that look alike

Workers in many groups
wear uniforms to look alike
and to show what groups they belong to.

Policemen and firemen in the city
wear uniforms when they work.

Football players and baseball players
wear uniforms that show what team
they belong to.

At a major-league baseball park,
all the ushers dress alike, too.

Airlines have uniforms for their
stewards and stewardesses
and for their airplane pilots,
copilots, and flight engineers.

78

Uniforms for special service

Royal Canadian Mounted Police parade
on horseback in Canada.

Policemen, guards, and servicemen wear
colorful uniforms in many parts of the world.

This is a guard in the
Vatican in Rome, Italy.

This man at the Tower of London in England
is called a Yeoman Warder or Beefeater.

Soldiers, sailors, marines,
coastguardsmen, and airmen
wear their dress uniforms
in parades.

Men of the Greek Guard
stand watch at the Tomb
of the Unknown Soldier
in Athens, Greece.

In India, soldiers of the
Camel Corps are part
of the cavalry.

Straps, pockets, and belts

When some people work, they wear clothes with straps, pockets, and belts. Can you tell who wears what?

Find the carpenter, the electrician, and the telephone lineman.

Who wears bib overalls like these with a long thin pocket for a folding rule and a special strap for a hammer?

Who wears a belt with pockets and straps for screwdrivers, pliers, and nippers?

Who wears a thick leather belt with a big steel ring on each side and a safety belt hooked onto the rings?

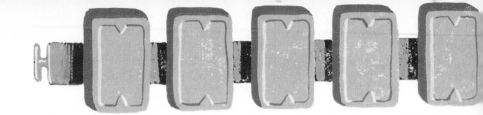

Find the deep-sea diver, baseball umpire, the policeman, and the soldier.

Who wears a belt with blocks of lead all around to help keep him under the water?

Who wears a black suit coat with pockets so big they hold half a dozen baseballs?

Who wears a belt like this with a pocket called a holster, with small leather loops for bullets, and with a metal ring for a billy club?

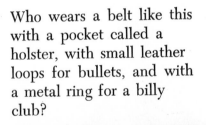

Who wears a wide cloth belt with holes at the top and the bottom for hooking on a spade, a canteen, and a first-aid pack?

Badges, patches, and sashes

You know that a policeman wears a badge. It helps show you that he is a policeman. A sheriff also wears a badge to show you who he is.

Their badges are one kind of insignia. Insignia are things such as special buttons, badges, and patches of cloth that tell you something about the people who wear them.

The insignia that the soldier in the picture is wearing on his uniform can tell you many things about him.

These service ribbons show the decorations and medals he has won. This badge and his shoulder patch show the unit he belongs to—recruiting. His job is to get other men to join the Army. He is a staff sergeant. He has been in the Army for nine years. Each stripe stands for three years.

Sailors, airmen, marines, and many others also wear insignia on their uniforms.

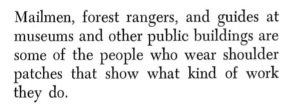

Mailmen, forest rangers, and guides at museums and other public buildings are some of the people who wear shoulder patches that show what kind of work they do.

Airline pilots and stewardesses wear "wings" that show what their jobs are and what airline they work for.

Railroad conductors wear lapel buttons that show what railroad they work for.

Medals and badges can be worn on a sash, too. Some Scouts wear the badges that they have earned on a sash. So do queens, kings, presidents, and other important people.

Queen Elizabeth II

Work gloves

Gloves that help save lives

Doctors must be careful when they operate. They must make sure that their hands are free of all germs. Otherwise, germs might get into the cut or wound and harm the patient.

Right before an operation, a doctor scrubs his or her hands and arms for at least eight minutes. The doctor's hands are clean, but he still wears gloves.

These special gloves are skin-tight so that a doctor may move his fingers easily. Doctors' gloves are made of rubber or plastic. They come in packages that are sterile or free of all germs. After a doctor uses a pair of gloves, the gloves are thrown away.

Rubber gloves mixed with lead

People who give X rays in hospitals and doctors' offices often wear gloves made of rubber mixed with lead.

Too many X rays can be harmful because X rays can go through almost everything. But they can't go through lead. That's why people who give X rays wear gloves made of rubber mixed with lead.

Rubber gloves that stop shocks

Electricians work with electric wires. Electricians must be very careful, because the electric current, which goes through the wires, can give a painful shock. So electricians often wear rubber gloves because electricity cannot go through rubber.

Boots and spurs

A cowboy's job is to take care of cattle. Boots help a cowboy do some of his work.

Why do cowboys wear high heels?

Sometimes the cowboy has to ride his horse for a long time. The high heels on his boots help him keep his feet in the stirrups.

Why is the heel of the boot slanted?

When a cowboy is on foot and lassoes a horse, he has to pull back hard on the rope and try to keep from getting dragged across the ground. That's when his high slanted heels help him. The cowboy digs his heels down into the dirt to keep his feet from sliding.

turkeyneck

Mexican

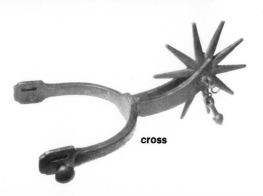

Why do cowboy boots have pointed toes?

Sometimes the cowboy has to mount his horse in a hurry to catch a running calf. That's when the pointed toes on his boots help him. They make it easy for him to put his feet into the stirrups without looking.

Spurs help the cowboy do some of his jobs

Sometimes a cowboy has to start his horse fast to catch a cow or calf. With his spurs he can poke his horse into a fast run in a hurry.

When a cowboy is on a bucking horse, he wants to stay in the saddle. So he sometimes wears spurs with small hooks. He slips the hooks under the wide strap that holds the saddle on. The hooks help him stay in the saddle instead of getting dumped on the ground.

There are many kinds of cowboy spurs. Here are some of them:

cross

eagle

89

Spikes for climbing

To do their jobs, some people have to climb where it is slippery and dangerous. They strap spikes to their boots so that their feet won't slip.

Climbing mountains

A mountain guide takes climbers up steep mountains. Sometimes he leads them over ice. Sometimes he leads them over snow that is packed and slippery.

If their feet slip, they might fall. And no one wants to fall off a mountain!

That's why mountain guides and mountain climbers wear steel spikes strapped to their boots. They call the spikes "crampons."

To climb, they stamp their crampons down into the hard snow and ice so that they won't fall down. Up the mountain they go, step by step.

Climbing telephone poles

Part of a telephone lineman's job is to work with wires and cables. The lineman has to climb tall wooden telephone poles. He also has to be able to stand on the pole while he works.

Why doesn't he use a ladder? Because a ladder would slow him down in his job. Instead, a telephone lineman wears climbing irons that are attached to his boots. Wearing climbing irons is like wearing a ladder on his feet.

Climbing irons are metal frames with spikes attached that fit on a lineman's boots. The spikes are so sharp that a lineman can "walk" up a wooden telephone pole by digging his spikes into the wood.

Look at the telephone pole near your house. Are there little holes in it? They were probably made by the lineman's climbing irons.

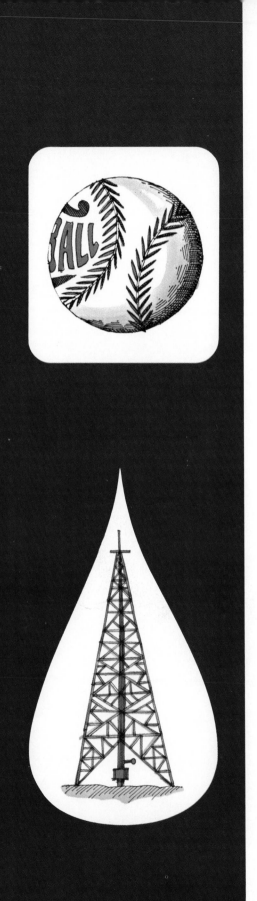

Made for You

Have you ever kicked a cow,
slept on a goose, or worn milk
on your feet and sheep on your back?
Sure, you probably have,
but you didn't know it.

Many things that you use, wear,
and play with are made by people
from things you never thought of.

Turn the page and you will learn how
you have probably used a cow,
a goose, milk, a sheep,
and other things
without ever knowing it.

mixing

filling tubes

How does toothpaste get into the tube?

STEENVELD

To get toothpaste out of a tube, you take OFF the cap and squeeze. But to get toothpaste into a tube, a machine puts ON the cap and squirts. The secret is that the machine squirts toothpaste into the tube through the tube's bottom.

Hundreds of toothpaste tubes stand upside down on a long moving tray. As each tube passes the place where the filling spout is . . . *Squish!* Just enough toothpaste comes out of the filling spout to fill the tube. Another tube moves under the spout—then another—and another. The spout fills each tube as fast as you can blink an eye.

Then the filled-up tubes move past a part of the machine that is a pincher. It pinches the bottom of the tubes and clamps them shut. Then each tube is boxed and sent to a store. There, your mother can buy it. Now with a squeeze and a squirt of the tube, you are ready to brush your teeth.

Sop it up!

If you have ever used a true sponge to wash anything, you were using a skeleton —the skeleton of an animal sponge that once lived in the sea.

Probably, though, the sponges you use were made in a factory. They are man-made sponges that had to have holes put into them so that they work like true sponges.

synthetic sponge mixture

To make the holes, sponge makers use the crystals of a special salt. They mix the crystals with other chemicals, and they heat the mixture. As it gets hot, the mixture gets thicker, and the crystals melt. Wherever a crystal melts, it leaves a hole.

After the mixture becomes a sponge, it is washed, dried, and cut into smaller sponges ready to be used.

cutting slabs of synthetic sponge

Why
do sidewalks
have cracks?

"If you step on a crack, you'll break your back."
That isn't really true. It is just a saying. Cracks
are in sidewalks for a good reason.

The cracks are grooves that the sidewalk maker
puts into the sidewalk before it dries. As the
concrete dries, water dries from the top of the
sidewalk faster than from the middle. And, as
concrete dries, it shrinks. So, the top of the sidewalk shrinks faster than the rest of the sidewalk,
and cracks form.

The grooves that you see in the sidewalk are called
control joints. They are placed so that the cracks
will form in straight lines—just the way the sidewalk maker wanted them to.

How pins get to be pins

How would you like it if someone straightened you, cut you, whammed you, ground you up, and boiled you? That's what a pin has to go through before it gets to be a pin.

Pins are made from reels of wire. A machine straightens the wire and cuts it into pin-size pieces. Another machine whams one end of each piece into a flat pinhead, and grinds a sharp point on the other end. Then the pins are poured into a boiling mixture that covers them with a thin coat of tin. After a wash and a polish, the pins are pinned to pieces of paper, ready for you to buy.

A safety pin is made from wire, too. But to be a safety pin, the wire gets bent in half, a loop is twisted in its middle, and a cap is pinched tightly on its head!

straightening wire for pins

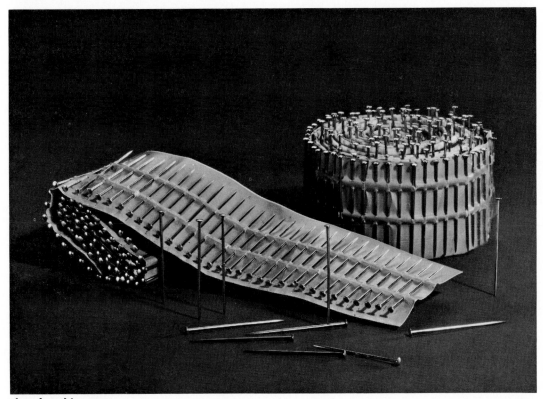

pins pinned to paper

101

Balls of string

If you tied a box together with a leaf, the leaf would wilt and fall apart. But when you use string to tie a box, you are really using part of a leaf.

The leaves of sisal or henequen plants are used to make string. A machine presses and squeezes the leaves until all that is left are thin threads, called fibers. Another machine pulls the fibers into even thinner threads. Then other machines and people comb, spin, and twist the threads until they hold together and become a long piece of string. As the string is made, still other machines wrap it onto a giant spool. Now it is ready to be cut and wound into smaller balls of string.

string fibers

twisting threads into string

pills

winding

A ball of string

Imagine playing baseball with a ball of string. If it started unwinding, it could get tangled around all the players. But you do play with a ball of string every time you play baseball. It doesn't unwind because a cover is glued over the string.

People who make baseballs first wrap some rubber skin around a tiny ball of cork. Then they cover the cork with a bouncy red rubber cover. They call this the "pill."

Then they start winding string around the pill. They wind and they wind, and they keep winding until they have a ball of string that is almost as big as a baseball.

After smearing the string with special glue, they sew on a cowhide or horsehide cover. They make sure the ball weighs between 5 and 5¼ ounces (140 and 149 grams) and is between 9 and 9¼ inches (22.9 and 23.5 centimeters) around. Now it's an official baseball. It won't unwind when it cracks against a bat and bounces across the ground or flies over the fence for a home run.

gluing

sewing

What's in a pillow?

Twenty-four geese packed in a bag would make a prickly, lumpy, leaping pillow. It would be noisy, too. But if you had the feathers from these geese, you could make a soft, plump pillow to curl up with at bedtime. Goose and duck feathers make the best pillows. The feathers are mixed with down, a soft fluff found beneath the birds' feathers. Then, the feathers and down are cleaned and sewed up in a bag.

But you can sleep on whipped rubber instead of feathers. Foam rubber pillows are made of latex, the sap of rubber trees. The latex is whipped until it is like cream. A chemical is added. Then, the mixture is poured into a mold to thicken. Next, it is heated, causing little pockets of air to form in the rubber. After cooling, the soft, bouncy rubber is covered and sent to a store.

Wax and string

One kind of candlemaker takes a string and dips it into a pot of melted wax. He dips it once, he dips it twice, he dips it again and again. Soon the string is covered with a thick coat of wax. *And this wax around a string is a candle.*

Another kind of candlemaker takes a pot of melted wax and pours it into molds shaped like half a Christmas tree, or half a snowball, or half of any mold. When the wax is hard, he takes the halves that match from the molds. He cuts a groove along one half of the candle for the string. Then he smoothes a little hot wax on each half and presses them together. *And these wax halves with string between them are candles.*

Still another kind of candlemaker takes a pot of melted wax and pours it into a machine full of long holes. He fills one hole, he fills two holes, he fills all the holes. Then he pushes a long string down the center of each hole. When the wax hardens around the string, a machine presses the wax out as long sticks. *And these wax sticks with string stuck through them are candles.*

melting wax

dipping string

handmade candles ready for drying

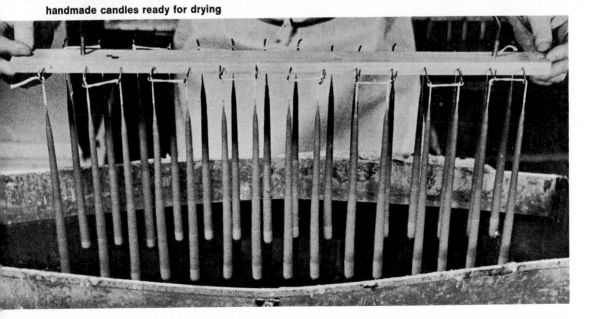

Black, white, and read all over

What is black, white, and read
all over? A book!

Books are printed and put together
at printing companies. These
companies use machines called
printing presses to print the
pages of books like this one.

Books may be printed in different
ways. This book was printed on
a press using rubber rollers and
ink. The rollers press against
the paper running between them.
The inked roller prints words on
the paper.

Then machines fold, gather, and
cut the pages after they come off
the press. The pages are sewn
together, shaped, glued, trimmed,
and finally covered.

printing *Childcraft*
binding *Childcraft*

Dots make pictures

Do you see dots before your eyes when you look at the picture on this page? You would if you looked at the picture through a strong magnifying glass.

When pictures are printed in books, the patches of color and the shades of gray are really many, many tiny dots.

The picture on the next page shows you how dots make a clown's face. Where the colors of his face are light, the dots are far apart. Where the colors are dark, the dots are close together.

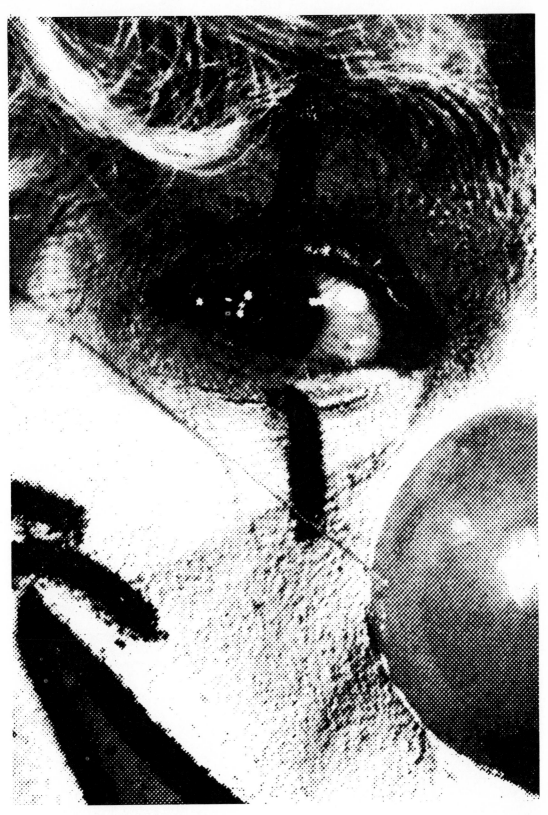

shaping pot on potter's wheel

plates and bowls ready for the oven

Baking pots
and plates

A pot is not a pot until it is baked.
It is just a flabby piece of clay
that has been shaped like a pot.

The people who shape the clay
and bake it into pots and dishes are called potters.

First, a potter carefully removes all the grit
and pebbles from the clay so that the clay
will be as smooth as it can be.
Then he mixes water with the clay
until the clay is the right thickness
for holding a shape.

Then the potter flops a lump of clay
onto a table that spins around and around.
The table is called a "potter's wheel."
As the clay whirls around on the potter's wheel,
the potter shapes the pot or dish
and rubs it smooth with his fingers and thumbs.

When the pot or dish is shaped
the way the potter wants it to be,
he sets it aside to dry.
Then he pops it into an oven and bakes it
until it is hard.

Sometimes potters mix a special clay,
called China clay,
with special stone, called China stone.
The dishes they make from this mixture
are the ones we call "china."

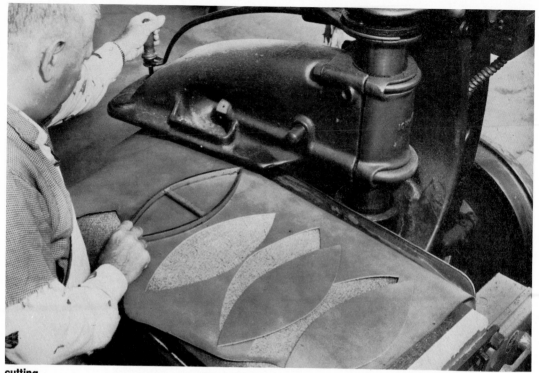

cutting

sewing

testing

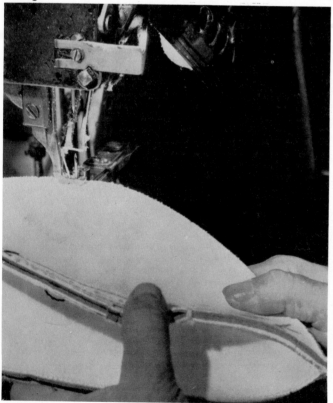

Kick the skin of a cow

When you kick a football, some people say you're kicking a pigskin, but you're really kicking the skin of a cow.

A football is often called a pigskin. That's because footballs once were made of pigskin. The name stuck, even though footballs are now made of cowhide.

At a football factory, people use machines to cut out pieces of cowhide and fabric lining. Each football is made of four pieces of cowhide. The cowhide and the lining are sewn together, inside out. Then, through a small opening, a worker carefully turns the sewn pieces right side out. Next, he pushes a rubber-like bag inside the opening and tightly laces up the opening.

Finally, an inspector pumps air into the bag. Then, he checks the football to make sure it is ready to be shipped to stores.

putting plastic yoyos together   stringing yoyos

Spinning wheel

Who can walk a dog, go around the world, and go over the falls
without taking a step? You can—if you have a yoyo. Yoyo tricks
have funny names.

Plastic yoyos are made from four pieces of plastic. There are two
outer shells and two inner disks. Each inner disk is pressed into
its outer shell. A metal bar or axle is stuck in one half. Then the
halves are joined. A string is put on and the yoyo is ready to spin.

Wooden yoyos take more time to make. They are carved by a
machine from a block of wood. A slot for the string is then cut
into the round piece all the way around. The yoyo is sanded,
painted, strung, packaged, and ready for you to walk a dog, go
around the world, or go over the falls.

The things our feet wear

What has a tongue, a heel, a toe, and lots of little "eyes"? A shoe, of course! But before it gets these parts, a shoe is just a strip of leather or canvas.

Machines cut the leather or canvas into shoe-shaped pieces that shoemakers can stitch, glue, and nail together to make a shoe. A shoe with a toe for kicking a ball, a heel for scuffing the dirt, eyelets for holding shoe laces, and a tongue for stopping the laces from pinching your foot.

Some shoes are cut out by hand.

Others are cut by machine.

A plantation worker taps a tree for latex.

Milk for galoshes

Did you know that we can get milk from a tree?
Tree milk looks like cow's milk
and smells something like cow's milk,
but we do not drink it.
This kind of milk is called latex.
And that's where rubber comes from.

A plantation worker called a tapper
uses a hooked knife to make a small cut
in the bark of a rubber tree.
He puts a spout into the cut
and places a small cup under the spout.
The latex drips into the cup.
Later he collects the cups of latex
from all the trees.
Then the latex is poured into big trucks
that look like milk trucks.
The trucks take the latex to rubber factories
where they make galoshes, tires,
rubber gloves, electric plugs,
and many other things out of rubber.

Slabs of thickened latex go through
rollers that press it into thinner sheets.

Toys made from coal and gas

These lumps of plastic were made from coal and gas.

A yellow truck and a pink baby doll. A blue boat and a red fire engine. Many toys are made of a hard, brightly colored plastic called polystyrene. Polystyrene was once black coal and a gas you can't even see!

Coal is dug from the ground. Natural gas is pumped out of the ground. Both coal and natural gas can be changed into many different liquids and gases. One of the liquids that comes from coal is called benzene. One of the gases that comes from natural gas is called ethylene.

A plastics factory buys benzene and ethylene. The benzene and ethylene are mixed together into a liquid. Chemicals are added to the liquid and it is heated. It becomes hard and clear, like glass. Now it is polystyrene. If the plastics manufacturer wants the polystyrene to be colored, powdered paint is added to the liquid before it is heated.

The hard plastic is put into a machine that grinds it up into tiny lumps. A plastics molding factory buys big bags or boxes of these lumps and turns them into toys.

The ground-up plastic is heated until it turns into a thick liquid. A machine pushes the hot liquid into molds of trucks or dolls or boats. In less than a minute the liquid in the molds cools and becomes hard. Then the colorful plastic trucks, dolls, and other toys are ready to be sent to stores where you can buy them.

Lumps of plastic are put into a molding machine. The plastic is heated until it becomes liquid. The liquid is pushed into molds and cooled. When it cools, it gets hard again. Out of the molds come toy racing-car bodies.

Toys of many shapes and many colors are made of plastic.

Making the clothes you wear

"Baa, Baa, black sheep" had three bags of wool. But do you know how the wool got off his back and into the bags? He got a haircut from a man called a sheepshearer.

A sheepshearer uses electric clippers with cutting blades that jiggle back and forth. The clippers buzz beneath the sheep's woolly coat. And the wool falls off.

electric clippers

People who make clothes for us have to cut, too. Men called cutters cut many layers of cloth at once with an electric cloth cutter that looks like a saw.

To make shoes, men use cutting machines to cut leather to the right size and shape.

Hat makers use cutting machines to trim hats evenly all around.

A tailor cuts with scissors and shears. Long scissors, with bent handles, are for cutting the cloth without lifting it from a table. Short scissors are for snipping off loose threads. Pinking shears are for cutting zigzag edges. Zigzag edges are strong.

Stripes, dots, and flowers

How do stripes get onto a shirt? How do polka dots get onto a handkerchief? How do flowers get onto a dress? Colors and designs are put on cloth in much the same way that words and pictures are put on this page.

A big printing machine made of rollers prints flowers onto the cloth. Each roller has a design or picture cut on it. When cloth goes through this printing machine, each roller prints its part of the design in color.

To print red polka dots, the rollers have tiny circles that are filled with red dye. To print green stripes, the rollers have grooves that are filled with green dye. But to print flowers, one roller with yellow dye puts on the flower centers. Another with red dye puts on the flower petals. Still another roller with green dye puts on the flower leaves. The cloth passes over all the rollers, and all the parts of the flower are printed on it. Now the cloth can be made ready to sell.

From caterpillars to cloth

Silk is a beautiful, shiny cloth made from the silk threads of caterpillars. We call the caterpillars silkworms. But they are not really worms. They are special caterpillars.

Silkworms make silk by oozing a liquid from holes near their mouths. The liquid gets hard and forms silk strings when it hits the air. Silkworms spin the strings of silk around their bodies. Soon, the worm looks like a mummy. All you can see is its case of silk or its cocoon.

Silkworms must be killed or they will burst from their cocoon and break the silk into small strings. They are killed with heat. The cocoons are then soaked in hot water. This makes it easier for people and machines to unwind the cocoons. The strings of silk are wound round a reel. Workers then twist the silk into thread, bundle it up, and send it to people who make the thread into cloth.

silk factory

Thousands of cocoons are piled on the floor of the factory.

close-up of cocoons

Silkworms spin their cocoons
in about three days.

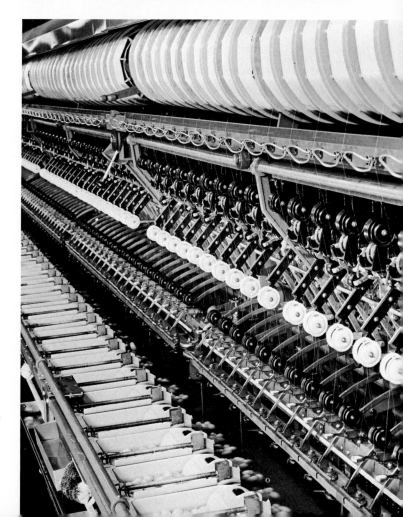

reeling machines

Each reel unwinds several cocoons
at one time, so that the thread will
be thicker and longer.

Sticking together

A stack of animal bones, ears, tails, skins, hoofs! What good are they? Most glues were once made from these animal parts. Today, only a small amount of glue is made from animals. Stronger glues and cements are made mostly from chemicals.

White glue looks like milk. It should. A part of milk called protein is used to make it. This protein, plus a sticky material from certain plants, is mixed in large kettles with other powders and liquids. Water is added. The gooey mass is boiled until most of the water is gone. The glue that is left will mend furniture, dishes, and even leather.

Rubber cement is made from real or man-made rubber. Other liquids are mixed with it. Be careful! Its fumes can harm you.

rubber cement

Turning a pebble into a jewel

The diamonds you see in jewelry stores are bright and clear and sparkling. But when diamonds come out of the ground, they look like dirty, grayish pebbles. Men called diamond cutters turn the gray pebbles into flashing, beautiful jewels.

The first step in turning a diamond into a jewel is to cut it in two. But a diamond is so hard that only another diamond can cut it. So the diamond cutter uses a saw that is coated with diamond dust. It is the diamond dust that really does the cutting.

When the diamond is cut in half, the two pieces are shaped somewhat like pyramids. The diamond cutter grinds the edges of the pyramids until each pyramid is round and smooth, like a tiny ice-cream cone. Then he grinds many little sides, called facets, onto each cone. The facets reflect light up through the top of the diamond. Now it flashes and sparkles with a rainbow of colors. The gray pebble has become a brilliant jewel!

Before a diamond is cut,
it looks like a shiny pebble.

A diamond is cut with a round saw
that is covered with diamond dust.

A cut and polished diamond
is a bright, flashing jewel.

135

Hotheads

I am a hothead.
If you rub me the right way,
I'll flare up.
What am I?

Once I was part of a tree.
But someone cut down the tree.
The tree was cut into boards,
and the boards were cut into millions
of little sticks.
So now I'm just a little stick.

But I'm a special kind of stick.
First machines sprayed me
and all the other little sticks.
The spray was a special chemical
that would make me burn evenly.
Then machines dipped one end of me
into a goo that was made out of
other chemicals.
When the goo dried,
it was ready to catch fire quickly
if someone rubbed it
quickly against the side of a matchbox.

That's right. I'm a safety match.
But remember—*be careful with me.*
I'm a hothead!
If you rub me, I'll flare up!

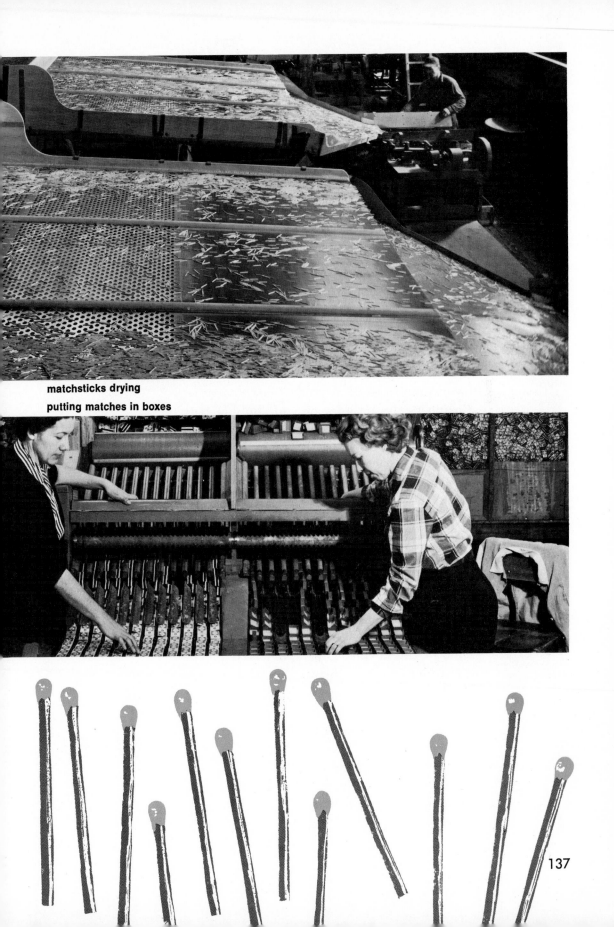

matchsticks drying

putting matches in boxes

137

Golden bubbles

You'd be surprised
if you found pieces of gold
sticking to the bubbles of your bubble bath.
But some men find gold pieces on bubbles,
and they're not surprised at all.

These men work with a special bath.
It is one of the ways
they separate gold from rocks called gold *ore*.

To make this special bubble bath,
the men mix oil and chemicals into a huge tank of water.
Then the gold *ore* is put into its "bubble bath,"
and a machine blows air into the tank,
making air bubbles form.
Some of the chemicals coat the gold pieces
so the gold sticks to the air bubbles.
The bubbles carry the gold pieces
to the top of the "bubble bath"
where the bubbles—and gold—are scooped up.

The gold pieces then are melted
and cast into gold bars called *bullion*.
Just one of the gold bars
is worth thousands of dollars.

casting pieces of gold into gold bullion

bars of gold stored at Fort Knox in Kentucky

This glass-blowing machine makes drinking glasses.

From sand to glass

Have you ever poured yourself a *sand* of milk? No, that sentence isn't wrong, because the glass you pour your milk into is made mostly of sand.

Glassmakers cook a mixture of fine white sand and two white powdery chemicals known as soda and lime. The mixture is cooked in a huge furnace that is so hot that the mixture melts into a liquid form of glass.

The melted glass then goes into a glass-blowing machine that blows and shapes hundreds of drinking glasses in a few minutes.

Then the drinking glasses take a trip on a long metal belt that carries them through a long oven. But this oven is different from most ovens. In this oven, the glasses are first heated, then cooled so they will not be brittle and easy to break.

Glasses travel to an oven, where heating and then cooling will make them strong.

glass blowing

baking

From a gob to a jar

A gust of air can muss your hair or blow a sailboat across a lake. But a gust of air can also blow a gob of molten glass into the shape of a jar.

In a jar-making factory, a gob of red-hot molten glass drops into a metal mold. The mold presses the gob of glass into the rough shape of a jar. *Whoosh!* A sudden gust of air squirts into the mold and blows the rough shape into a smooth jar.

After the jar has cooled slowly, it is ready for pickles or olives or chocolate-covered ants or anything else that comes in a jar.

cooling

Bottles and jars come in different sizes and shapes.

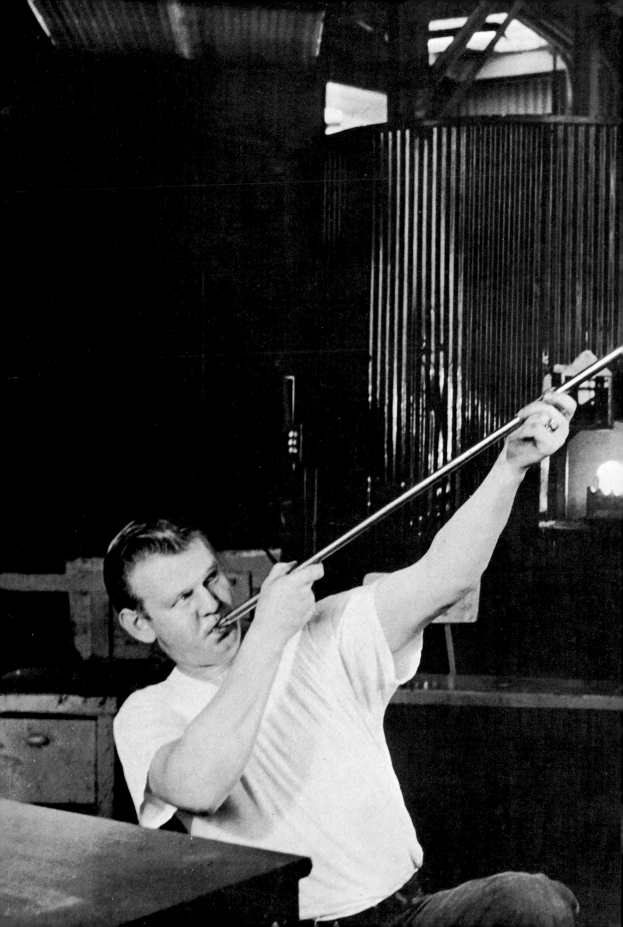

A pipe for blowing glass

A man called a glass blower uses a long blowpipe
to make different shapes of glass.
He can make a bottle, a fancy vase, a glass swan,
or a little glass elephant.

First he puts his blowpipe into a furnace
to get a gob of glass.
The glass is very hot and looks like thick syrup.
He has to turn his pipe
to keep the glass from dripping.

He puffs and blows air into the pipe,
and a bubble of glass comes out the other end.

He uses other tools
to poke, cut, and pull the bubble
into different shapes.

When he wants to make many bottles
of the same size and shape,
he uses a hollow frame or mold.
He puts the hot glass into the mold
and blows into it with his pipe.

Metal for building

Aluminum is a strong, light metal. It is made in a big steel box called a cell or a pot. There, the aluminum is so hot that it is a liquid. Workers let it flow from the cell into a ladle that has a handle. Then they tip the ladle to pour the aluminum into molds where it can cool into shapes called pigs.

Steel is heavier than aluminum. It is an alloy or mixture of iron and other materials. At a steel mill, steel scraps are melted in a huge furnace. Then the hot steel is poured into molds to cool.

Most large buildings are made of steel beams. They are held together by metal bolts called rivets. One construction worker heats each rivet until it is red-hot. Then he picks it up with a pair of tongs and tosses it to a man called a holder-up. The holder-up holds out a scoop, catches the rivet, and puts it through a hole in the metal.

How to bake a brick

Bricks are made of mud. But if they are made of mud, then why don't they squash when you pile them up to build a house? Why don't they crumble when you walk on them or drive a car over them? They don't squash or crumble because they are made of a special kind of mud, called clay, that is cooked in an oven.

Brickmakers grind the clay and mix it with water until it is a gooey mass. A brickmaking machine pushes the gooey mass through a hole. And when the mass comes out of the hole, it looks like a thick ribbon of clay. Another machine, called a brick cutter, cuts the clay ribbon into brick shapes. Then the brickmakers shove them into big ovens called kilns. In the kilns the bricks bake and become hard enough not to squash or crumble.

cutting

baking

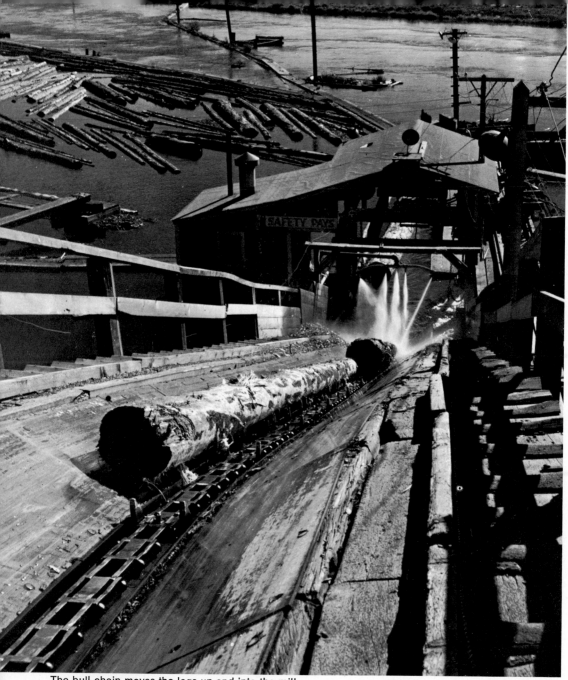

The bull chain moves the logs up and into the mill.

From logs to lumber

At a large sawmill, you can hear
the thumping and bumping of rolling logs,
the chugging and grinding of moving chains,
and the screeching and screaming of whirring saws.

A sawyer cuts a log into many boards.

The workers who run the saws at a sawmill
are called *sawyers*.
The head sawyer looks at the logs
after a big moving chain moves them into the mill.
He decides how the logs should be cut
to make the best lumber.
He works sawing machinery that saws
each log into huge rough boards.
Other sawyers in the mill run machinery
that cuts the rough edges from the boards,
makes the edges of the boards square,
and cuts the boards to the right length.

Trimmer saws make the
boards smoother and smaller.

Toothpick trees

You don't pick toothpicks from trees, but you do have to pick the trees from which toothpicks come.

Toothpick makers choose white birch trees. White birchwood is strong and white. It doesn't have a bad taste as some other woods do.

Toothpick makers put long pieces of birchwood into boiling water or scalding steam to soak the bark off and to make the wood soft.

One machine cuts the long pieces of wood into toothpicks. Another machine sharpens the ends of each toothpick. Then it puts the toothpicks into a steam oven to dry.

When the toothpicks are dry, they shower into a barrel full of chalk that tumbles back and forth. The chalk smooths and shines the toothpicks. Another machine counts them and puts them into a box.

toothpick sheets

tumbling toothpicks

packaging toothpicks

Logs from dust

Some people burn "logs" that aren't real logs at all. They are log-shaped lumps made from the sawdust left over at sawmills.

The people who make sawdust logs first mix the sawdust with a special kind of glue.

Then they push the sticky sawdust into a machine that blows the sawdust into a hot mold. The mold squeezes, scrunches, and packs the sticky sawdust tightly together into the shape of a log.

When the mold cools, a rod in the machine rams against it, pushing out the log. At the same time, the rod pushes in more gluey sawdust for another sawdust log.

Now the log-shaped lumps are ready for you to buy and burn in your fireplace.

sawdust piles
pressing logs

House skeletons

Without your bones you couldn't stand up. You would flop to the ground like a puppet without strings. A house without a skeleton would tumble down, too. The skeleton of a house isn't made of bones though—it is usually made of wood.

But before a house skeleton is made, it needs something to stand on. So housebuilders pour concrete to make a foundation. Then carpenters hammer and saw and put together pieces of wood to make the skeleton. They fasten the skeleton to the foundation with big metal bolts. Now the skeleton is ready for its skin. Not real skin, but skin made of pieces of wood, sheets of asbestos, and rolls of tar paper to help keep the house warm in the winter and cool in the summer.

Putting color in paint

Paint gets its color from a powder called pigment. Pigments are made from ground-up rocks, or coal, or tar, or chalk—even from clay. Different kinds of pigments give different colors.

To make paint, pigment is put into a big mixing machine filled with special oils. The pigment and oils are mixed together into a lumpy, colored paste. The paste runs through rollers that make it smooth. A liquid called thinner is mixed into the paste, turning it into a thick liquid. Now it is paint.

Paint gets its color from
colored powders called pigments.

Pigment is mixed with oil
in big mixing machines.

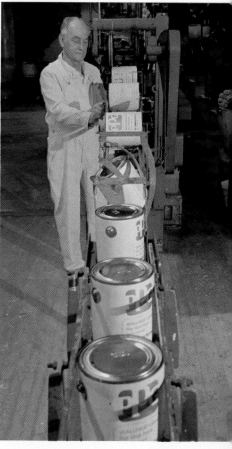

The oil and pigment are now
colored paint. Put in cans,
the paint is sent to stores
where it will be sold.

159

Concrete = w + c + s + g

Can you guess what to mix
together to make concrete?
Mix water and cement and
sand and gravel.

Cement is a fine, gray
powder that gets like
paste when water is added.
Sand and gravel make
cement stronger.

Where is concrete mixed?
It can be mixed by hand,
but a cement-mixer truck
is used for big jobs.
This truck has a big
barrel on its back.
As the truck moves along,
the barrel mixes the cement
with sand, water, and gravel.

The barrel turns—
rumbledy-grind.
And when the truck gets
to where it is going—
PRESTO!

The mixture is ready to
be poured for a driveway,
a sidewalk, or a road.
When the mixture hardens,
it is concrete.

glass tubing

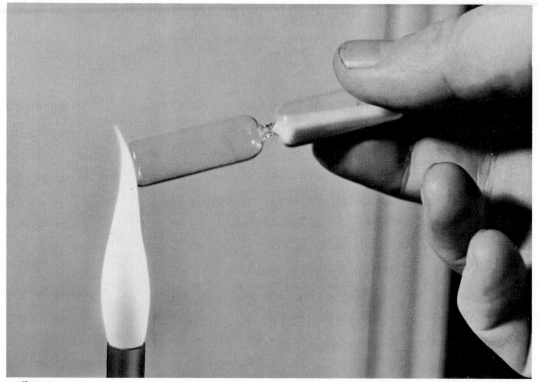

sealing
162

How did the "sand" get in?

You need three minutes to cook a soft-boiled egg. Without looking at a clock, how can you tell when the egg is ready? If you have an egg timer, you can watch how long it takes for the tiny sandlike grains to trickle through the tiny opening between the top part and the bottom part. When all the grains trickle through, three minutes have passed.

Companies make egg timers with machines or by hand. Either way, they buy tubes of glass from glass companies.

When egg timers are handmade, a worker heats the middle of a glass tube until it softens enough to stretch. He stretches the tube until the glass in the middle becomes about as thin as a needle. After the middle cools, the worker heats and pinches one end of the tube. Again he lets it cool.

Now the worker pours just the right amount of tiny grains into the open end of the tube. The grains trickle through the tiny middle and into the closed end of the tube. To complete the job, the worker heats and closes the other end of the tube.

PAUL McNEAR

P. McNEAR

Drilling for oil

The oil that people put in cars and burn for heat
comes from big, underground oil pools.
Once, these pools were the bottoms of ancient seas,
where millions of plants and animals lived and died.
Mud, sand, and rock covered
the dead plants and animals.
And slowly, over millions of years,
the dead plants and animals turned into oil.

Men who work for oil companies
try to find these ancient sea bottoms.
They drill deep holes where they think oil may be.
If they find a pool of oil,
the oil is brought up out of the ground by pumps.
Then it is stored in huge tanks
until it is sent to a refinery.
There, it is cleaned and made ready for use.

huge oil tanks

close-up of drill bit

Getting Help

If you see a fire, whom do you call?
If you need help at school,
whom do you ask?
If you are sick,
whom does your mother call?

There are firemen, teachers,
doctors, and other community helpers
where you live.
Getting help is easy
when they are nearby.

The next few pages are about people
who help us.

A policeman's beat

A patrolman is a policeman who protects a certain neighborhood.
That neighborhood is called his "beat."

At night he checks the doors of stores on his beat to make sure
they are locked.

He helps lost children find their way home.

Policemen patrol some neighborhoods in a car. They report accidents or trouble to the police station over a two-way radio in their car.

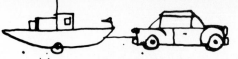

Traffic policemen

A policeman directs traffic at busy street corners so that people and cars can cross safely.

He protects children on their way to and from school.

A policeman or a police-woman checks parked cars.

At a parade, policemen hold back crowds of people.

Sometimes a policeman on a motorcycle turns on his siren and chases someone who is driving too fast.

Finding help

United States

England

It is easy to find help wherever you may be. Policemen wear special uniforms to let you know who they are.

City policemen in the United States usually wear blue. They often wear brighter colors while directing traffic so that people may see them easily.

Policemen in England are nicknamed "bobbies." They wear blue uniforms and blue helmets.

France

Canada

Australia

Spain

Hats will often show you whom to ask for help. In northern Australia, policemen wear broad-brimmed hats. Spanish policemen wear hats with pointed corners. And round, flat-topped hats are worn by the police in France.

Policemen in Canada are easy to spot. Their pants have a wide gold stripe on each leg. Their hats have a matching gold band.

Some policemen in Italy wear boat-shaped hats with feathers. Traffic policemen in South America wear white hats called pith helmets.

Italy

No matter where you are, you can usually tell a policeman by his uniform. Helping hands are always nearby.

South America

Firemen on the land

Firemen have many special jobs at a fire.
Some attach hoses to fire hydrants
and to the pumper truck.
Some hold the hoses and shoot water on the fire.
Some chop holes in the roof and smash windows
to let out smoke and gases.
Some climb ladders and carry down people
trapped inside the burning building.
Some hold canvas life nets so that people
who are trapped can jump to safety.

Firemen
on the
water

Firemen use boats
to fight fires
on lakes and rivers.

176

Firemen in the sky

Firemen called smoke jumpers parachute from airplanes to fight forest fires.

Sometimes firemen in airplanes drop chemicals that help put out fires.

Firemen to the rescue

Clang! Clang! Clang! Clang! The firemen are ready when the alarm rings in the fire station. If the firemen are on the second floor, they slide down a shiny, slick pole. There is no time to come down the stairs.

The firemen put on their helmets, rubber boots, and rubber coats. Then, they jump on the fire truck to ride to the fire.

A fireman's helmet has one lining for warmth and another for protection.

A fireman is protected as he fights the fire. His helmet has a brim that catches water, keeping the fireman's neck from getting wet. His helmet is lined, too. It keeps him warm and protects his head from falling objects.

Fire fighters at an airport wear plastic masks. The masks cover their faces and protect them from splashing, burning gasoline.

Part of a teacher's job is to ask questions that help boys and girls learn to think.

In school

To help you learn, a teacher does the work of many people.

A teacher is a listener when you read from books. A teacher helps you to say new words.

A teacher is a storyteller who reads about kings and queens, pilots and airplanes, cowboys and Indians.

A teacher may be a speaker of a foreign language. A teacher listens to you in language lab and helps you learn to speak the foreign language correctly.

A teacher may be a musician who plays the piano and teaches you songs.

But most of all, a teacher is someone who helps you to learn as much as you possibly can.

Language labs allow students to speak and to listen to a foreign language.

Outside the classroom

A teacher watches you while
you play on a climber
during recess.

She is a guide when she takes
you to places such as the zoo.

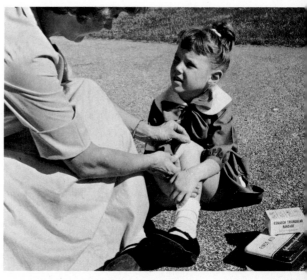

She is a nurse when she puts a
bandage on your skinned knee.

When you have a problem, she
tries to help you solve it.

After school

A teacher's day often does not end when the last bell rings. A teacher may work after school to do many things.

A teacher reads books and magazines to make sure that you learn the right things in the best way possible.

A teacher corrects papers after school and keeps a record of your work and attendance.

Some teachers even go to school after school. They attend classes at a nearby college.

Parent-teacher meetings are often held after you leave school, too.

Need help after school? Ask your teacher.

A parent-teacher meeting gives your teacher a chance to meet your family.

Teachers at college

College teachers are usually busy. They study
and search for new things to teach.

Teachers at college speak to their classes about people,
places, plants, plays and poems, and just about everything.

They often write books. They also give speeches at
meetings and at other colleges.

But most importantly, college teachers help college
students learn to find the answers to questions themselves.

In the library

Librarians help you find out about almost anything.
They help you find books that you might like.
Sometimes they tell stories.
Sometimes they read aloud.
Sometimes they show movies.
Librarians will even help you put on a play or puppet show.

Sometimes librarians show movies.

Librarians enjoy reading stories aloud.

In public libraries

A public library has books, magazines, and newspapers for everyone.

Some libraries have record players and tape recorders
so that people can listen to records and tapes.

A librarian helps people find what they would like to read.

She chooses records they would like to hear.
She shows people how to find out things from globes and maps.

When someone wants to borrow a book
to take home,
a librarian's helper checks it out for him.

A librarian uses a big filing cabinet
called a card catalog.
In it there are drawers
where she keeps cards
that show where to find the books
that are in the library.

Libraries that move

Have you ever seen books travel down a street
or fly through the air or roll down a hallway?
They can.

Bookmobiles are libraries on wheels. Librarians
use them to take books to people who do not have
a library nearby.

Bibliocopters are helicopters that bring books
to small, out-of-the-way villages in Russia.
These books help the village people know what
life is like in other places.

Hospitals have moving libraries, too. Book
carts are wheeled around to the patients who
must stay in bed.

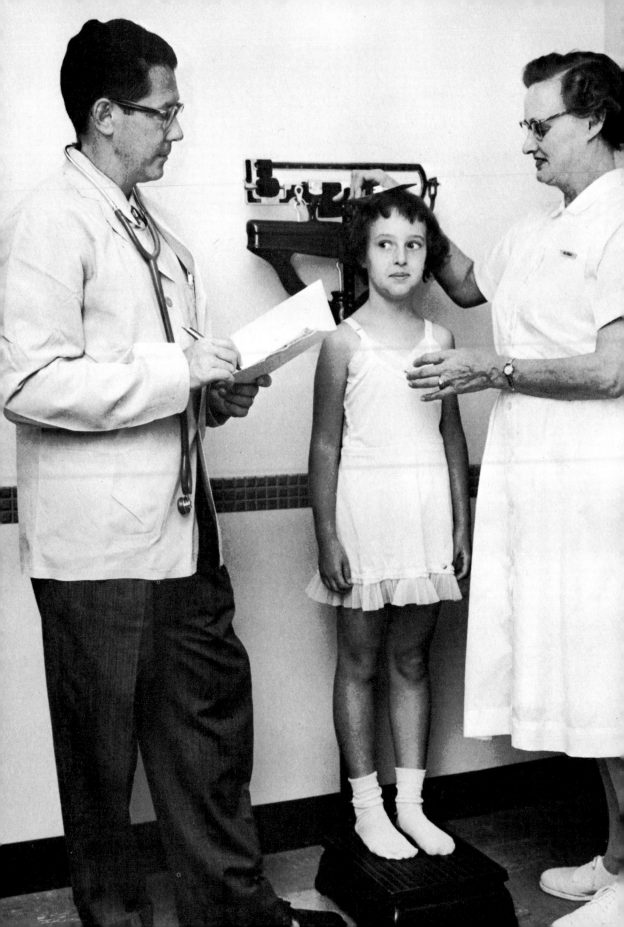

In the doctor's office

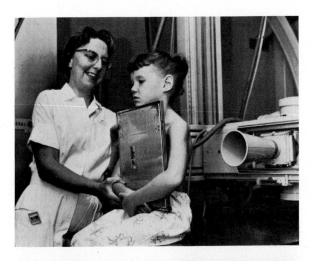

Sometimes a doctor
sees patients in his office.

A nurse weighs the patients
and gets them ready for the doctor.

If someone has a bruise or a sprain,
sometimes the doctor takes X rays
to see if any bones are broken.

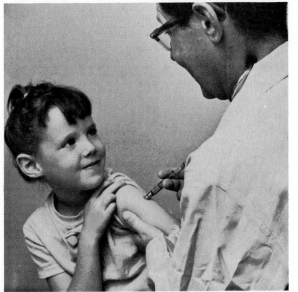

The doctor gives shots
to many people
to keep them from getting
whooping cough and other diseases.

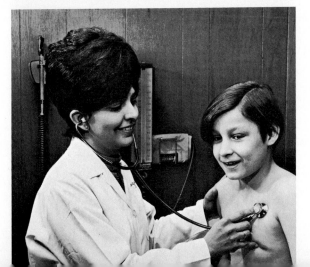

Even when you are not sick,
you may go to a doctor's office
to be examined for school
or for camp.

Doctors in the hospital

When a sick person needs special care,
the doctor sends him to a hospital.

When there is an accident
and someone gets hurt,
a doctor calls for an ambulance
to take the person to a hospital.

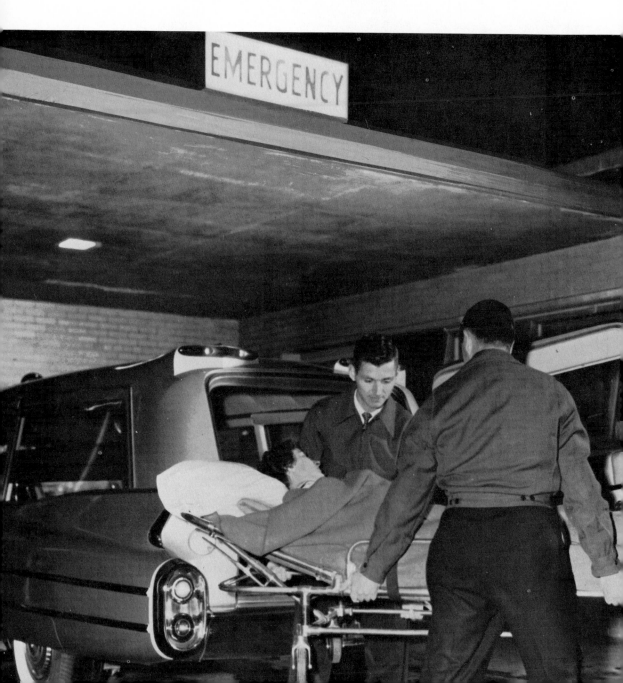

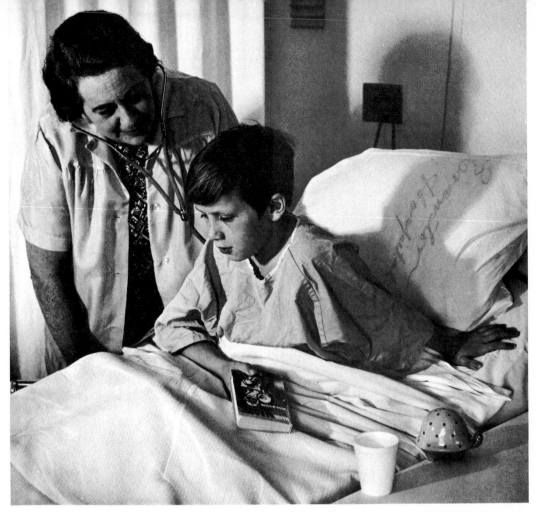

Family doctors
check their patients
who are in the hospital.

Some doctors at the hospital
teach students
who are studying to become doctors.

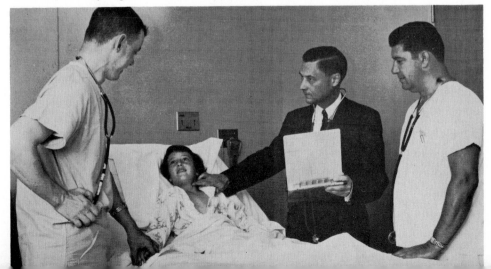

At the dentist's office

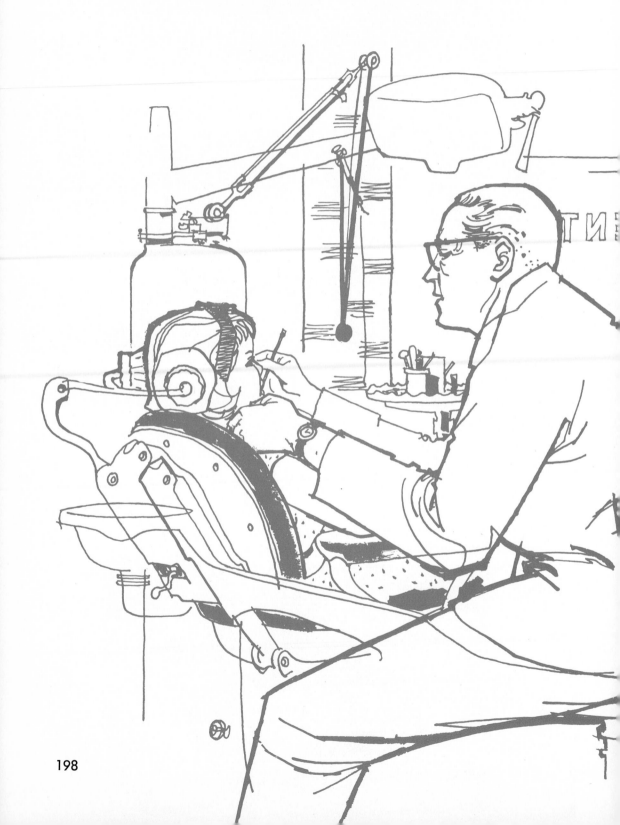

At the dentist's office you sit in a special chair. The dentist can tilt the chair or make it move up or down or around.

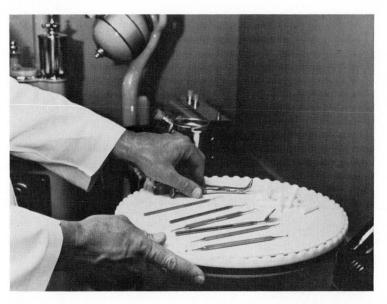

The dentist uses many small tools to help him see if you have any cavities or soft spots in your teeth.

Sometimes the dentist uses an X-ray machine to take a picture that will show him whether the insides of your teeth are healthy.

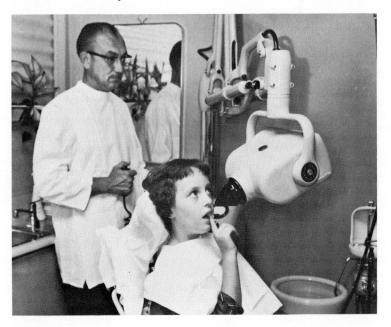

Cleaning your teeth

When the dentist cleans your teeth, he uses a little round brush and a special tooth powder.

The dentist shows you how to keep your teeth clean. Sometimes he uses a big set of false teeth and a big toothbrush to show you how to brush your teeth the right way.

Brush all over, using short, back and forth strokes.
Brush the inside part of your front teeth up and down.

If you have a soft spot in a tooth, the dentist cleans the spot away with his drill. Then he fills the tooth.

The dentist straightens teeth

Sometimes a dentist straightens teeth that are crooked. To do it, he puts braces on the teeth. The braces are small wires and little pieces of metal. After the teeth are straightened, he takes off the braces. The teeth look better. And they chew food properly.

A dentist makes false teeth

Sometimes a dentist makes false teeth for people who have lost their real teeth.

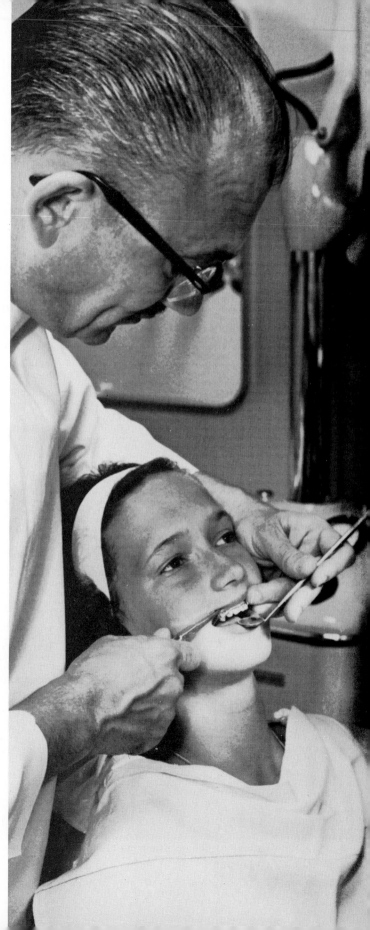

Ministers, priests, and rabbis

Ministers, priests, and rabbis are leaders of their religious groups. Ministers belong to the Protestant faith and priests to the Roman Catholic faith. Rabbis belong to the Jewish faith.

Priests, ministers, and rabbis are often called clergymen. These people of God conduct services in their churches and synagogues. They teach about God and how to be a better person.

At the part of the Mass called the Consecration, a priest prepares to bless the bread and wine.

In a synagogue, a rabbi reads from the Torah.

A minister preaches a sermon at Sunday service.

Clergymen preach sermons and perform many other services at special times in people's lives.

Ministers and priests baptize babies and grownups. They also confirm children and adults.

Rabbis conduct a ceremony called *bar mitzvah* for Jewish boys and *bas mitzvah* for Jewish girls.

And when a man and woman marry, the wedding is usually performed by a minister, priest, or rabbi.

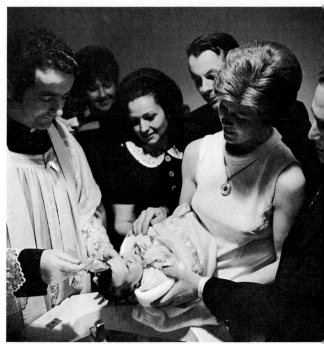

The godparents hold the baby, and the parents watch while a minister baptizes the child with water.

A cantor and rabbi take part in a boy's *bar mitzvah*, on or near his 13th birthday.

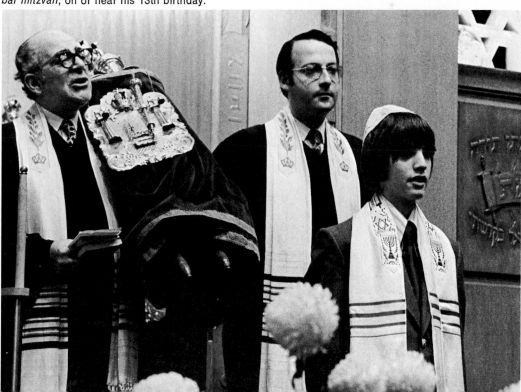

Giving help

A minister visits an elderly man recovering at home from an illness.

The leaders of different religions often help people outside their church or synagogue. They may be called on day or night to comfort sick or dying persons at home or in a hospital.

When a person dies, clergymen try to ease the sorrow of the family. They also hold funeral and burial services for the dead.

Nuns are women who dedicate their lives to religion. They often work in hospitals, teach in schools, and get food for the hungry and clothes for the poor.

Young people join a priest at a meeting.

Along with clergymen, nuns work in other areas, too. Sometimes, they meet with city leaders to talk about community problems and to work on special projects.

Nuns and clergymen work with young people. They help the teen-agers plan meetings and parties.

They also help people in trouble. Nuns and other religious leaders listen to problems, give advice, and sometimes recommend special help to those who need it.

A nun watches over young children at a day-care center.

Schoolchildren listen and talk to a priest.

Chicago's water filtration plant is on Lake Michigan.

Washing water

How do you know that the water that comes from your faucet is clean? It *is* clean, but people had to clean it for you first.

It may seem impossible to wash water. But water can be washed. Here's how! Rain water and water that may be dirty comes through pipes to a place called a filtration plant. At the filtration plant the water pours through fine sand. As the water seeps deeper and deeper, the chemicals, germs, clay, and tiny animals that are in the dirty water get caught on the grains of sand.

Then *drip, drip, drip.* Out comes clean water! Water to cook with. Water to clean house with. And water to drink and wash yourself with.

Water flows through layers of sand and pebbles before reaching the pipe at the bottom.

Clean water, food, and air for the city

People want the water they use
to be clean and pure.
But most cities get water
from lakes and rivers.
This water must be made safe.

First, chemicals are added to
help remove some dirt and germs.
Next, the water is run through a
filter of sand and gravel
to take out the rest of the dirt.
Then, more chemicals are added
to kill the last germs.
Sometimes the water is sprayed
into the air to make it
taste and smell better.

Now the water is safe for everyone.

City food inspectors
see that food is safe to eat.
They also inspect restaurants,
markets, dairies, and other places
where food is handled to see
that these places are clean.

Many cities hire men and women
to check on air pollution.
These inspectors work
to help keep the city's air clean.

What's under the manhole cover?

Mice, snakes, and many other creatures often crawl into holes. But did you ever see a man crawl into a hole?

In the middle of some streets you will see a round, flat piece of iron. It is a manhole cover. And underneath the cover is a dark, dark hole. Someday you may see a man come and put a little fence around the hole, and then climb down into it.

He turns on his flashlight and sees all kinds of pipes and cables. There are pipes that carry water from the water station to all the houses on the street. There are pipes that carry gas from the gas company to all the houses on the street. And there are telephone wires and cables that carry electricity from the electric company to all the houses on the street. But what is the man doing down in the hole? He is either fixing the pipes and cables or putting in new ones.

A small fence keeps people from
falling into an open manhole.

A workman comes
down into the manhole.

In the manhole, the workman
fixes some telephone wires.

Keeping the city clean

City cleaners keep the city clean.
They help make the city a healthy place to live.

Some keep parks and playgrounds clean.
Others clean streets and gutters.
In the winter they spread sand or salt on icy streets
and take away the snow.

213

Brushes that clean streets

At night, when the streets are not busy and when most of the city is sleeping, it is time for the street cleaner and his truck to go to work.

The street-cleaner's truck has big brushes on it. He has to steer carefully, and stay close to the curb, so that two wire brushes at the front of the truck can spin dirt out from the gutter.

That dirt, and more dirt that is on the street, gets whirled up into the truck by a big plastic brush that turns around and around at the back.

During the daytime, some street cleaners walk around and pick up litter from the streets. They push long, flat brooms along the gutters. Then they shovel the rubbish into a cart or a trash box.

Taking away
city trash and dirt

Some city cleaners collect garbage and trash
from homes, stores, and factories.
Then they take it away to be burned and buried.

Other city workers
clean the dirty water
that comes from sewers.
They work in a building
where machines and chemicals
clean the dirt from the water
and kill the harmful germs in it.
Then the water is safe to throw away
without getting rivers and streams dirty.

How's the weather?

A weatherman works with many meters to find out about the weather.

To see how hot or cold it is, he uses a thermometer to take the temperature of the air.

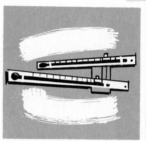

thermometer

One way he finds out if the weather is going to be fair or stormy is to measure the pressure of the air. To measure it, he looks at a meter called a barometer. If the barometer shows that the air pressure is high, the weather probably will be clear. If it shows that the pressure is getting low, the weather probably will be cloudy or stormy.

barometer

When a weatherman talks about the humidity, he is talking about how much water vapor is in the air. To find out what the humidity is, he uses a meter called a hygrometer.

hygrometer

When he wants to know how fast the wind is blowing, he uses a meter called an anemometer. To find out which way the wind is blowing, he looks at a dial connected to a weather vane.

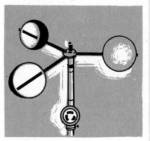

anemometer

Getting Across

Sue's grandfather is coming
for a visit.
She read it in a letter.
Kip knew it was going to rain today.
He heard it on the radio.
Ann loves horses.
She draws and colors them
as her hobby.

How do people let their thoughts
and feelings be known?
They use pens and pencils,
newspapers and letters,
crayons and chalk, radio and TV.

The next few pages will let you know
how we get things
that make it easier to get
our ideas across to others.

strings of graphite

inserting graphite

cutting

packing

Writing with graphite

When you want to draw a picture or write a word, you probably use a pencil. Where do pencils come from? Pencil makers grind clay and a material called graphite together into a mixture that looks like dough. They pour this mixture into a machine that has small holes. Another machine presses down on the mixture to push it out through the holes. It comes out in long strings that are put into an oven to dry.

After the strings are dry, the pencil makers lay them inside grooves in a wooden block. Then they glue another wooden block over the strings. Next, they send the blocks through a machine that cuts them into shiny, new pencils.

Rub it out!

Marks from pencils can sometimes show up in places where you don't want them. The marks might ruin your drawing or letter. What can you do? Rub them out!

Erasers are made of latex, the juice of rubber trees. Latex is soggy when it comes from the trees. So, machines squeeze out the wetness until the latex becomes a hard lump of rubber.

Other machines press and roll the lump until it becomes a big block. Still other machines cut the block into pieces that look like erasers.

But before the pieces can be used as erasers, they have to be heated. The heat fixes the erasers so that they won't get soft and sticky in summer, or hard and brittle in winter.

224

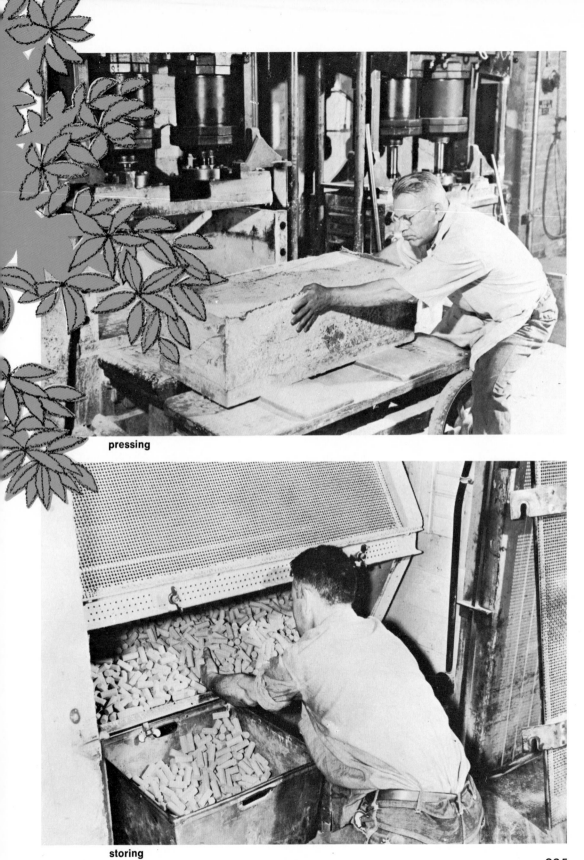

pressing

storing

Holes for writing

When you write with a ball-point pen, you are writing with holes. The tip is rough and full of holes.

The ball in a ball-point pen is made from millions of tiny bits of metal. A machine presses and squeezes the bits together into the shape of a ball—a ball full of holes. Then, the ink can ooze through the holes to put your thoughts on paper.

inserting ball in pen tip

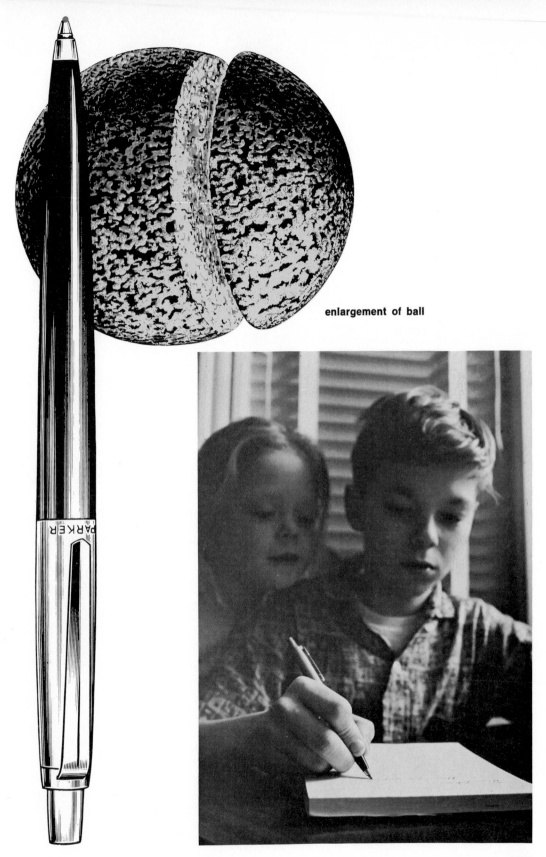

enlargement of ball

cutting

chipping

cooking

drying

What to write on

Drawing on walls might make others mad. Sending a letter on a stone slab would be expensive. Paper is the best place to write your words and draw your pictures. How is paper made?

First, papermakers cut wood into chips. Then the chips are cooked in a mixture of chemicals. The chips cook until they are a soggy mash called pulp. The pulp is rolled flat and left to dry into sheets of paper.

Paper is also made from used paper. This way saves trees and cuts down on pollution.

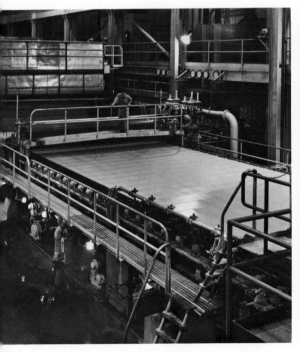

rolling

Writing with a rock

You're writing with a rock when you write with chalk! But it is a rock that was first crushed to powder before it was shaped into a piece of chalk.

Chalk makers mix the powder with other things. Then they pour the mixture into a mold that presses it into the shape of a stick. Sometimes the chalk mixture is squirted through the holes of a special machine that gives it the stick shape. After the chalk is shaped, it is baked until it is hard enough to use on a chalkboard.

Walls for writing

Your teacher often asks you to write on a wall at school. Of course, there is a chalkboard on the wall. Chalkboards make it easier for your class-mates to see what you are writing.

A chalkboard is made in a factory from a piece of steel. The steel is showered with a glasslike substance called porcelain enamel. A thin coat of this material covers the piece of steel.

The chalkboard moves on a long metal belt through an oven. It bakes until the coat hardens. Then it cools. After that, you can write on the chalkboard with chalk or a special crayon.

PETER STEENVELD

mixing
boxing

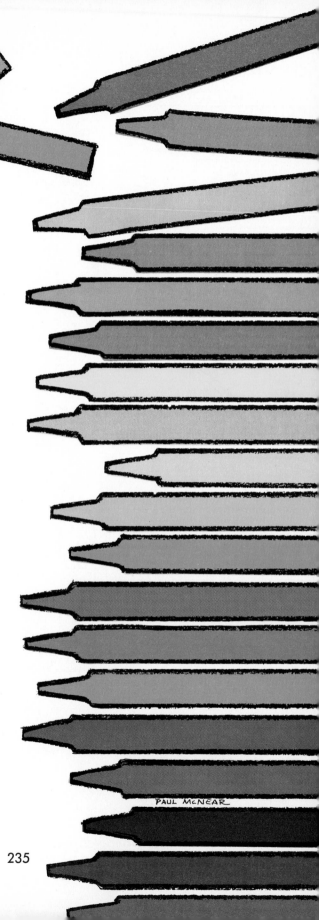

Colorful crayons

Drawing a picture? Making a sign? Why not use colorful crayons for both? Then everyone will notice the idea you are trying to get across.

Crayons begin as a glob of wax in a big cooking pot. A crayon mixer uses wax and powdered colors. He pours melted wax into a big mixing kettle. Then he dumps colored powder into the kettle. Big blades mix the wax and powder together.

When the crayon mixture is smooth, it is poured into a big tray with deep holes. The colored wax takes the shape of the holes. The wax is left to cool. When it is hard, the crayon maker pushes a handle on the tray to press the crayons from their holes. Then the crayons are labeled and put in crayon boxes.

PAUL McNEAR

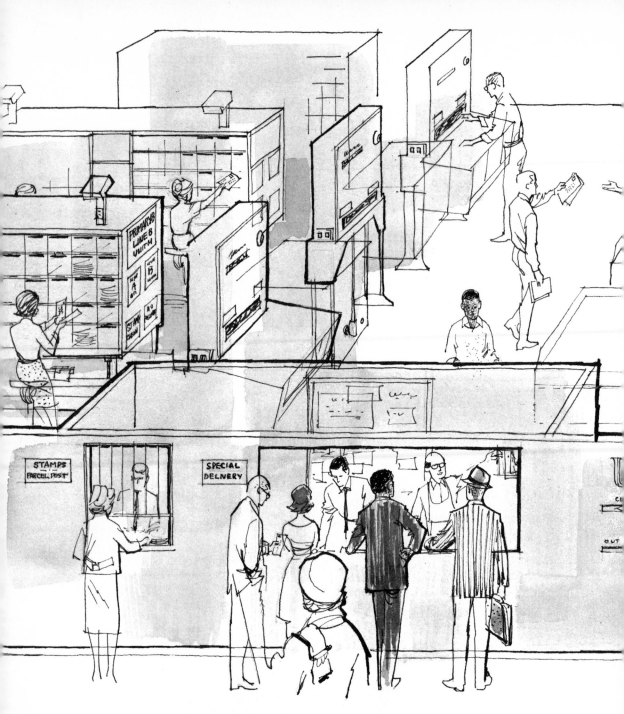

Moving the mail

What happens to your letter after you mail it?

Post-office workers make sure it gets
to wherever you want it to go.

Some sell stamps to put on letters and packages.

Some weigh packages so that people will know
how many stamps to put on the packages.

Some of the workers use machines to sort letters.
Others use machines to mark the stamps to show
that they have been used.

15 tons and what do you get?

Faster mail service. That's right. The post office uses a machine weighing 15 tons that moves mail quickly.

The machine is a letter-sorting machine or LSM. This machine uses a moving belt to bring the letters to a postal worker. The worker reads the address, presses a button, and the machine moves the letter to the right bin. Some post offices even have a machine that reads typed addresses.

A new set of sorting machines is being tested. These machines stack the letters, cancel them, and separate them. Incoming mail is sorted by these machines, right down to each postman's load of letters.

So, when you get a letter, think about the 15-ton monster that helped to deliver it.

An automatic address reader sorts outgoing mail. Workers tie the stacks of mail and place them in the correct shipping bin.

240

Postage-stamp pictures

Most postage stamps have tiny pictures on them. They may be pictures of presidents, or heroes, or new airplanes or rockets, or new states. The pictures may honor a special day, such as Independence Day, or the day when a city or country is one hundred years old.

Pictures on stamps may also honor a special event, such as the orbiting of a satellite, or the launching of a big ship, or the climbing of a high mountain, or the opening of a big fair, or the naming of a new country. Stamp makers choose pictures for stamps that show people, places, or things that a country is proud of. Look at the stamps on envelopes that come in the mail. Can you tell why each stamp got its picture?

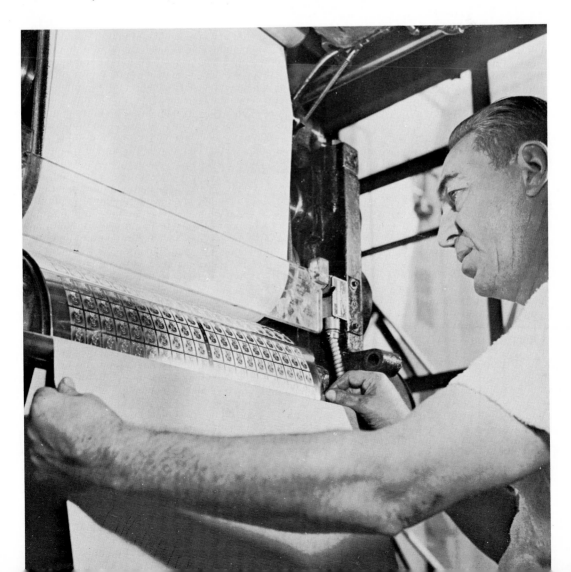

Japan

Spain

France

Delivering the mail

Mailmen work in many lands.
They deliver letters, papers, magazines, and packages.

They deliver mail to people in cities and towns.

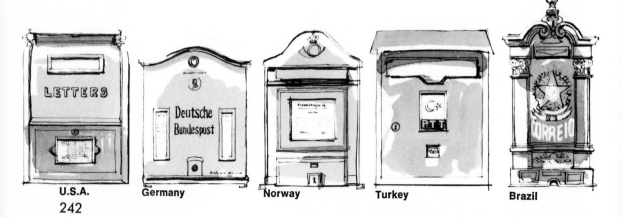

U.S.A.

Germany

Norway

Turkey

Brazil

242

They deliver mail to people in the country.

Some mailmen pick up mail at letter boxes
and deliver it to the post office.

Israel

In the television studio

People in a television studio
do many jobs to get ready for a program.

A lighting man fixes the spotlights.

A boom operator works a microphone
at the end of a long pole or "boom."

One cameraman takes a picture,
while another cameraman gets the next picture ready.

The floor director hears the director through earphones
and tells people what the director wants them to do.

The property man takes care of furniture
and things performers use during the program.

244   Stagehands put up the set for a show.

In the television control room

People in the control room
look into the studio through a big window.
They work the buttons
and machines that make a television picture.

The audioman
makes sure we hear the right sounds.

The video control man
makes the picture look right.

The switcher pushes buttons
to make the pictures go in the right order.

The director plans the pictures and the sound.
And the script girl makes sure
that the show is running on time.

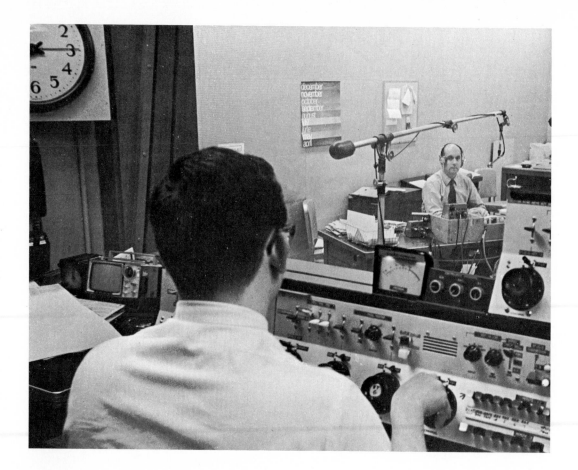

Disc jockeys

The voices you hear on many musical radio programs
belong to men or women called *disc jockeys*.
Disc jockeys play music on records, sometimes called *discs*.
Sometimes they play music and commercials
on special tape recordings, too.

When a disc jockey's program is broadcast,
his voice goes into a microphone.
He may talk about who wrote the music
and what orchestra or group is playing or singing it.
He may read a commercial.

At small radio stations, disc jockeys
plan their own programs, announce the music

and some commercials over a microphone,
and play the records or tapes.

At larger radio stations, many people work together
as a team to help a disc jockey.
One person may prepare the program and choose the music.
Someone in the music library gathers the tapes
that will be played.
The disc jockey looks over a list that tells him
the music, the commercials, and other announcements
he has to play on his program.
After he has his material, the disc jockey
sits near a microphone, ready to broadcast
his program.

Talking to and from cars

The two-way radio in a police car helps policemen to catch law-breakers and to help people who are in trouble. When the desk sergeant at a police station gets a call for help, he radios the police car that is closest to where the help is needed.

If policemen in a car need extra help or equipment right away, they use the radio to talk to headquarters. When policemen in one car are chasing someone, they can radio another police car to set up a roadblock.

After firemen put out one fire, sometimes they are called to another fire by two-way radio.

Firemen also use the radio to call headquarters when they need more firemen and more equipment to help fight a big fire.

Many taxicabs have two-way radios so the drivers can keep in touch with the central office.

When a customer telephones for a cab, a man or woman called a dispatcher talks to the cab drivers by radio. The dispatcher gives the order to the driver who is closest to the customer's address. Within minutes the driver is outside the customer's house.

Talking from the sky

When men who fly high in the sky have to talk with people on the ground, they use two-way radios with earphones and microphones.

Policemen in the sky

Some policemen watch traffic from airplanes or helicopters. When an air policeman sees a speeding car, he picks up a microphone to talk to policemen in a car on the ground. He tells them what kind of car is speeding so that they can catch it.

Policemen in helicopters also look for traffic jams as they fly back and forth over highways. If they spot a traffic jam, they radio for help to policemen on the ground.

Talking from outer space

An astronaut soaring through outer space talks into a microphone that is built into his space helmet.

He tells scientists on earth many facts, such as how he is feeling and how the instruments in the spaceship are working.

Pilot to control tower

Whenever an airplane pilot lands or takes off, he has to talk to people in a control tower.

If he has to make an emergency landing, he warns the control tower to get fire trucks and ambulances ready for action.

If he cannot land at an airport because of bad weather, the men in the control tower have to tell him where he can land. Sometimes the tower men radio the pilot to tell him he is approaching a bad storm. They tell him how to avoid it.

The pilot's earphones and microphone are important. He uses them to keep in touch with men on the ground.

Getting
the news

Newspaper workers help people find out
what is happening almost everywhere—
in their own town and in other parts
of the world.

Some of the workers are the newsboys
who sell newspapers on the street
and who bring the news to your doorstep.

Reporters and news photographers
are the workers who get the news,
write about it,
and take pictures of it.
They work in many parts of the world.

Reporters go to wherever something important happens.
They ask many questions—
Who? What? Where? When? Why? How?

Photographers take pictures
that help show the news.

Reporters talk with people to get the news.

In the newspaper office

Many editors and copyreaders work in a newspaper office. They read the stories, look at news pictures and cartoons, and write headlines. They decide what should go into the newspaper.

Sometimes a reporter goes to the office to write a story. Sometimes the reporter telephones the news to a rewrite man who types the story as he listens to the reporter.

News stories from reporters in other parts of the world come into the newspaper office on a teletype machine.

An editor takes the stories from the teletype.

In some newspaper offices, artists called cartoonists draw pictures about something in the news.

257

Getting ready
to print
the paper

When news stories are ready to print, editors send them to the composing room. There, men called typesetters use a machine to put all the words on pieces of metal called type.

Others get pictures ready. They use machines and chemicals to put the pictures on pieces of metal or hard plastic called plates.

Printers put the type and the pictures in metal frames called forms. Each form is for a different page in the newspaper.

Men called stereotypers use the forms to make thick paper molds called "mats." They use the mats to make curved plates of metal to put on the printing presses.

From the presses
to the newsstand

Pressmen start the printing presses.
Paper from huge rolls
at one end of the presses unwinds—
up, over, down, and under
row after row of whirling rollers.
At the other end of the presses,
out come the newspapers.

Men load the newspapers
onto waiting trucks
that speed them
to ships,
airplanes,
trains,
and to newsboys in the city.

261

Machines that answer

Computers are machines that give quick answers to difficult problems. For example, a computer can add up all the numbers in a big telephone book in the time it takes you to wink your eye. And a computer can add, subtract, divide, or multiply a million numbers in the time it takes you to button a button.

Of course, you could add up all the numbers in a telephone book, or even work out a problem with a million numbers. But it would take you from now till who knows when to come up with the right answers. That's what's so great about computers. They work fast—faster than you can snap your fingers, even faster than you can wink an eye.

Getting from Here to There

Trains and engineers,
buses and drivers,
airplanes and stewardesses,
ships and sailors.

These are some of the ways you travel
and some of the people who help you.
Turn the page.
You will learn how people and things
get from here to there.

The train
to Grandma's

Where is the engineer
who sits in the locomotive
and drives the train
that takes you to Grandma's?

Where is the fireman
who helps the engineer
who drives the train
that takes you to Grandma's?

Where is the conductor
who takes the tickets
on the train that takes you to Grandma's?

Where is the baggage man
who takes care of your suitcases
on the train that takes you to Grandma's?

Where are the cooks
who cook the meals
for the people who ride
on the train that takes you to Grandma's?

Where is the porter
who makes the beds
and keeps things clean
on the train that takes you to Grandma's?

Have a nice trip to Grandma's!

At the railroad station

Many people work at a railroad station to help people who are going on trips.

Ticket agents sell tickets and help people plan their trips.

The baggage agent takes care of baggage that will go into the baggage car.

A passenger agent checks
tickets to make sure people
get on the right train.

A redcap helps passengers
carry their suitcases.

269

To keep trains running

Before a train is ready for a long trip, mechanics and other workers get the locomotive ready in a shop or a roundhouse. At a roundhouse, railroad workers use a turntable to turn a locomotive around.

A brakeman sees that the cars are hooked together.

A dispatcher pushes levers on his control board to change signal lights along the tracks and to throw switches that steer trains onto the right tracks.

He decides when and where trains should leave stations, wait, and pass each other.

A track inspector makes sure tracks are safe.

When tracks need repairing, a group of men called the section gang repairs them.

Keeping track

Many railroad workers use earphones, loudspeakers, and microphones to talk to each other and to passengers.

At the railroad station

At a railroad station you hear a voice making announcements about when and where to catch the trains.

The man who makes the announcements talks into a microphone. His voice comes over loudspeakers so everyone in the station can hear him.

In the caboose

Every freight train has a conductor. He rides in the caboose at the end of the train.

To talk with the engineer at the front of the train, the conductor uses a two-way radio that looks like a telephone.

Over the hump

Railroad workers put freight trains together in a freight yard. In the yard is a little hill called the hump.

A worker near the hump talks into a portable radio called a walkie-talkie. He reads the number on each car to a switchman in a tall building called the tower.

The switchman checks a list to see which track the car should go on. He pushes a button to switch the car to the right track.

An engine slowly pushes the freight cars to the top of the hump. Each car rolls over the hump and down onto the right track.

Piggyback ride

What can ride piggyback on a train? The trailer of a truck!

Sometimes when crates of food are sent to different parts of the country, a truck carts the crates to a railroad depot. Men unload the crates and put each crate on the train. And when the train gets to where it is going, men have to unload the crates and put them on another truck. All this loading and unloading takes a long time.

So sometimes instead of unloading a truck crate by crate and putting each crate on the train, a driver drives the whole truck onto a flatcar of the train.

After unhooking the truck from the trailer, he drives the truck away. The railroad men tie down the trailer with chains. Now the trailer is ready for its piggyback ride.

When the train gets to where it is going, a truckdriver hooks the trailer to a truck and drives it and the crates to wherever they are going.

Here come the ships!

Ships loaded with cargo sail from harbors of their country to another country. And after the cargo is unloaded, the ships may return home with other cargo.

Ships from the United States carry coal and chemicals to West Germany and may return with machinery.

Ships from Brazil carry coffee and cocoa to the United States, and may return with coal and wheat.

Ships from the United States carry cars and trucks to India, and may return with tea and sugar.

Goods that go to other countries are *exports*. Goods that come from other countries are *imports*.

277

A ship and its crew

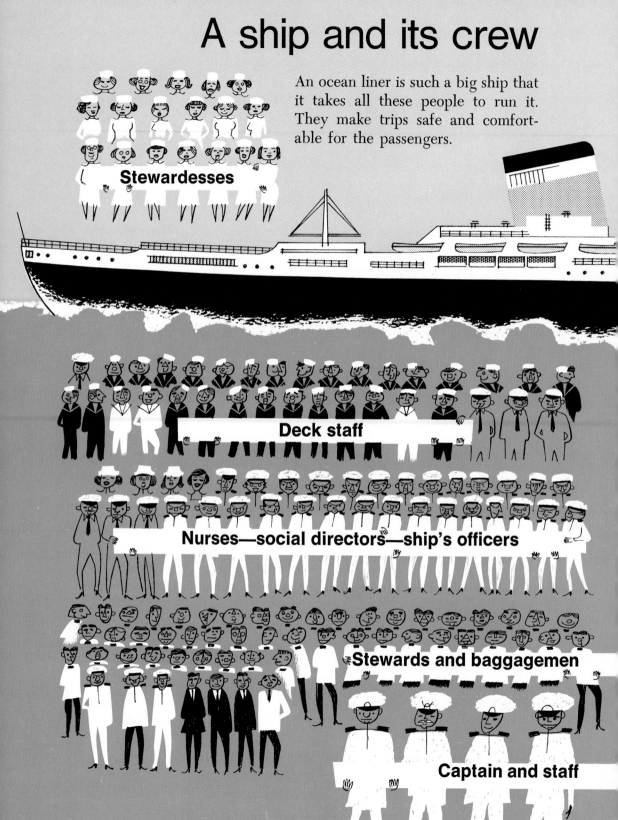

An ocean liner is such a big ship that it takes all these people to run it. They make trips safe and comfortable for the passengers.

Stewardesses

Deck staff

Nurses—social directors—ship's officers

Stewards and baggagemen

Captain and staff

278

Chefs

Assistant cooks

Engineering staff

Stewards and baggagemen

Captain's staff

The ship sails out

After tugboats pull the ship away from the shore and into the open sea, the captain orders, "Full speed ahead."

Radiomen keep in touch with people on land by sending and receiving messages.

In the engine room the chief engineer
and his men speed up the engines. They
make sure that the engines work right.

Telephone operators take care of telephone calls from cabin to cabin on the
ship. The operators can connect calls
from the ship to faraway parts of the
world.

The
captain
and
his
staff

The captain is in command of the ship, and he is responsible for everyone on board.

On the ship's bridge he talks into a speaking tube or a microphone to give orders to his men.

Deck officers take turns standing on the ship's bridge. From the bridge they steer the ship, they watch the sea and the sky, and they check instruments and charts.

Pursers are men who keep the ship's records
and check the passengers' tickets.

Sailors keep everything
on board "shipshape."

Water travel in other lands

In Venice the streets are canals filled with water. And the taxicabs are graceful boats called gondolas. A gondolier pushes his gondola with a long oar. An oar is a pole with a wide flat end.

A Turkish boatman uses oars to row his boat across a harbor.

A raft of coconuts is poled to market on a river in the Philippines. The men use their poles to push against the river bottom.

Here are two boatmen using long wooden poles to push their tublike boat down a river in Iraq.

These boatmen in northern Borneo are using paddles to move a tiny canoe pulling a string of palm-tree logs. A paddle is a short pole with a flat end.

An Eskimo uses a pole with a paddle on each end to push a kayak made of sealskins.

Going by plane

At an airport, many workers
help people who are taking trips by plane.

Skycaps, or porters, help people carry
their suitcases into the terminal.

In the terminal, some airline workers
weigh the passengers' luggage.

Some sell tickets and
some check passenger lists.

A passenger agent announces
when people may board the plane.

286

Seats for sale

If you plan to fly to New York on Friday,
and fly back to Chicago on Sunday,
you have to telephone an airline for a reservation.
An airline agent, who answers your call,
has to find out what time the airplanes leave and arrive,
and if there are seats available on the planes.
If there's room, she makes a reservation for you.

In large cities, major airlines get
thousands of telephone calls every day for reservations.
One airline agent can answer about 200 calls in a day.
And that's easy because an agent uses computer machines
with buttons on them.

All she has to do is push the correct buttons
for a particular flight on a particular day,
and the information appears on a card.

With the machines, she can find out most of the information
that she needs in less than a second.
Then she can tell you the information.

Before you grow up, maybe an airline agent
will be able to answer 400 calls a day
with the help of a pushbutton machine
that gives information
on a TV-like screen.

Planning the flight

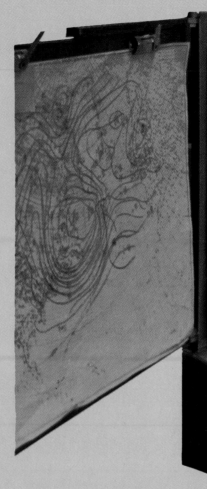

In an airline dispatch department, weathermen study the latest information about winds, clouds, and temperatures.

Pilots look at weather maps and make their flight plans.

A flight dispatcher helps the pilot plan the flight. After take-off, a radio operator will talk with the pilot by radio. Then he will let the dispatcher know where the plane is during the flight.

At every airport there is an air-traffic control tower. Inside, men direct all the landings and take-offs by radio, radar, and special lights.

Getting the plane ready

Before a plane takes off, many people get it ready for its trip.

A mechanic checks the engines and the instruments to see that they are in working order.

Cargo loaders put baggage, mail, and other supplies aboard the plane.

A truckdriver delivers food
that has been cooked
in airline kitchens.

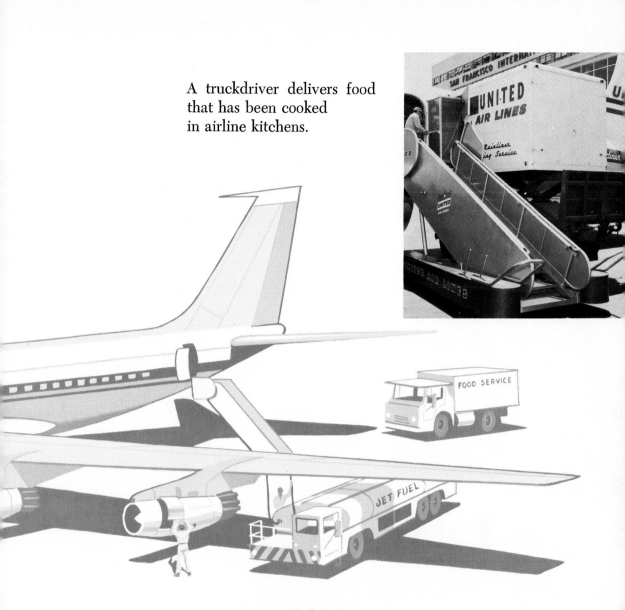

Men called fuelers
fill the wing tanks with fuel.

In the air

The pilot flies the airplane.
The copilot helps him.

The flight engineer
checks the equipment
and makes sure
it is working properly.

In the passenger cabin,
a stewardess serves meals
and makes sure
everyone is comfortable.

Rides for cars

You can go for a ride in a car, but did you know that cars can go for a ride, too? When new cars leave a factory, they go for a ride on a train or a truck. This is the way they are sent to the town or city where they will be sold.

On the trains and trucks, new cars are put on double-decker and even triple-decker carriers. How do the cars get to the second and third decks? First, men hook two narrow metal ramps on the back of the carrier. Then the cars are driven up the ramps to the top decks and parked. The men tie the cars down with chains so they won't fall off while the carriers are moving.

297

298

By car

Can you imagine going to a circus and seeing only cars? When cars were first invented, people did see them at circuses. They were new and strange then. But you probably see cars every day and ride in them almost as often.

If you travel by plane, train, or bus, you must leave when they do. But when you go by car, you can leave at any time. That is why there are so many cars. Most people like to come and go as they please.

Going by car is easy, but it is not free. Cars are expensive to buy and to keep running. A car must have gas and oil to run.

This means stopping often at a service station. And sometimes a car's engine must be greased or its oil must be changed.

By bus

What would it be like to be a bus driver?

You might drive a bus from street corner to street corner in a city. Your bus would have wide aisles for the riders who stand. The seats would be close together. Your bus would have two doors so passengers could get on and off easily. And right next to you would be a coin box. Clink, clink, clink—everyone drops their fare into the box.

You might drive a bus between cities. Your bus would have narrow aisles because riders aren't allowed to stand. The seats would be padded and the backs could be moved down for sleepy riders. Your bus would be air-conditioned. It would not have a coin box because passengers buy their tickets before getting on the bus.

Which bus would you like to drive?

City buses stop every few blocks to pick up passengers.

Long-distance buses travel between cities.

A stewardess serves a snack on a long bus trip.

Money

What is sometimes metal
and sometimes paper?
What is sometimes square
and sometimes round?
What is sometimes smooth
and sometimes bumpy?
What is sometimes saved
and sometimes spent?
What is sometimes kept
in machines with slots,
drawers, and buttons?

Money is the answer to all
of these questions.
Read on and see.

Can you?

Can you buy a piece of candy
in India for a *rupee*
or rent a gondola
in Italy for some *lire?*

Can you ride on a bus
in Mexico for a *peso*
or eat lunch
in Japan for some *yen?*

Can you buy
a box of toy soldiers
in England for a *pound*
or ride on a train
in Sweden for a few *kronor?*

Can you get a doll
in Russia for a *ruble*
or buy a bottle of pop
in France for a few *francs?*

Can you get a new hat
in Panama for *balboas*
or ride on a llama
in Peru for a *sol?*

You can because
a rupee,
a lira,
a peso,
a yen,
a pound,
a krona,
a ruble,
a franc,
a balboa,
and a sol
are the names of money
in these countries!

rupee

peso

krona

franc

balboa

sol

ruble

yen

pound

lira

305

stone money of Yap islanders

Unusual money

On Yap Island, coins were made of stone
and had to be carried on a pole.

In Africa, lumps of salt
were used as money.

In Malacca, tin coins looked like trees.
Each branch was a coin.
And people broke off the coins
as they needed them.

Bronze coins that looked like spades
were used in ancient China.

Gold money rings were used
in ancient Egypt.

Even today in Tibet,
bricks of tea
mixed with wood
are used as money.

coin tree

money ring

spade-shaped money

money bricks of tea and wood

307

Swapping for a top

I didn't have any money,
but I had a snail shell
that I swapped for a goose feather.
And I swapped my goose feather
for a marble with a chip in it.
But the marble would not roll,
so I swapped it for a lead soldier without a head.
But a soldier without a head cannot see,
so I swapped it for a ping-pong ball.
The ball would not bounce,
so I swapped it for a hard-boiled egg.
But I wasn't hungry,
so I swapped the egg for a jackknife.
The jackknife had a wiggly blade,
so I swapped it for a top.
A top is what I wanted,
and I didn't have to spend any money to get it!

100 PENNIES

Counting coins

If you could open your piggy bank and look at the coins, could you count them to find out how many dollars you have?

Two half dollars is a dollar, and four quarters is a dollar, and ten dimes is a dollar, and twenty nickels is a dollar, and one hundred pennies is a dollar.

But two quarters is a half dollar. And one half dollar and two quarters is a dollar.

Five dimes is a half dollar. And one half dollar and five dimes is a dollar. Or two quarters and five dimes is a dollar.

Ten nickels is a half dollar. And one half dollar and ten nickels is a dollar. Or two quarters and ten nickels is a dollar. Or five dimes and ten nickels is a dollar.

Fifty pennies is a half dollar. So one half dollar and fifty pennies is a dollar. Or two quarters and fifty pennies is a dollar. Or five dimes and fifty pennies is a dollar. Or ten nickels and fifty pennies is a dollar.

How many dollars you have depends on the number of coins you have, and the kinds of coins you have.

The pictures on a penny

Look at a penny. On one side of it, you can see the face of President Lincoln. You also see the words *In God We Trust*, a date, and the word *Liberty*. On the other side of the penny, you see a picture of the Lincoln Memorial and the words *United States of America*. You also see the words *One Cent* and *E Pluribus Unum*, which means "one out of many."

How do the pictures get on a penny? A machine cuts the round coin from a long ribbon of metal. These round coins are known as *blanks* because they have no pictures on them. Later, a machine called a *coining press* stamps a design or picture on each side of the coin.

Nickels, dimes, quarters, and half dollars are cut out and stamped with designs and pictures, too.

A machine punches out blanks that will later become pennies.

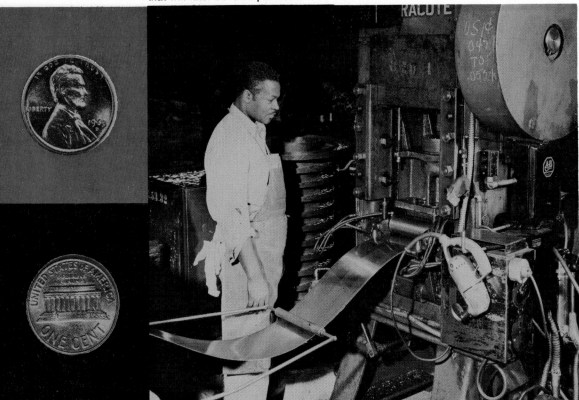

Blanks fall from the vibrator into a tank.
The vibrator is a machine that makes the coins level.

The edge of a dime

What's round and flat, has bumps on its sides, and ridges on its edge? A *dime!* But why does a dime have ridges on its edge?

Until recently one of the metals used to make a dime was silver. And silver is a valuable metal. Some people used to chip and scrape the silver from the edges of dimes. Then they would use the silver shavings to make other things.

The government of the United States put ridges on the edges of dimes so that people could tell when a dime had been chipped and scraped.

Today dimes are made of copper and nickel. But coin makers still put ridges on dimes because people are used to seeing them that way. Quarters, half dollars, and "silver" dollars have ridges for the same reason.

A high-speed press prints sheets of dollar bills.

The paper
in paper money

The paper in paper money of the United States is very special. No one but the federal government can use it. One of the special things about this paper is the tiny red and blue threads scattered in it. If you look closely, you can see the threads.

The paper is made from a blend of linen and cotton rags. Linen and cotton are both strong cloths, and this mixture makes the paper bills last longer. While the paper is being made, each sheet is counted again and again to be sure that no sheets are lost or stolen.

Washington, D.C., is the only place where the United States government prints paper money. In a building there, machines print paper money in sheets of 32 bills. Each sheet of paper is counted again and again. The sheets are cut into single bills, which are checked for printing mistakes and counted again. Then the bills go to banks.

Counting money

People who work in grocery stores, department stores,
and gas stations often use an adding machine
called a cash register.
A salesperson pushes the buttons on the register
to add up the things people buy.
A window at the top of the machine
shows a customer the amount of the sale.
And the amount is recorded on a paper tape
inside the machine.

Sometimes, people who work in offices
have to add up rows and rows of numbers.
To save time, most offices have adding and
figuring machines that add, subtract, multiply,
and divide numbers automatically.

A teller at a bank uses a machine with buttons
that counts money and figures out correct change.

A cashier at a movie theater presses buttons on a machine
that releases a customer's change into a little metal dish.

Machines that figure and count
save people time
and keep people
from making mistakes.

A letter called a check

Sometimes when your father buys a suit
he doesn't pay for it with money—
he writes out a check.

If you look at the check, you will see
that it has the name of a bank on it.
And your father has money in that bank.

When your father writes out a check,
it's like writing a letter to the bank—
a letter telling the bank to use his money
to pay for the suit.

Money in the bank

You may save your money in a piggy bank. When the piggy bank is full, you take the money to a big bank. You give your money to a person called a *teller*. Then you get a bankbook that tells how much money you have in the bank.

What happens to the money you put into the bank? The bank uses your money, and the bank pays you for the use of your money. The money the bank pays you is called interest. And the interest is added to the money you already have in the bank.

The bank lends your money to people who need it. These people borrow the money from the bank and pay the bank interest to use it. The bank uses this interest to pay you for the use of your money and to pay the cost of running the bank.

What's Economics?

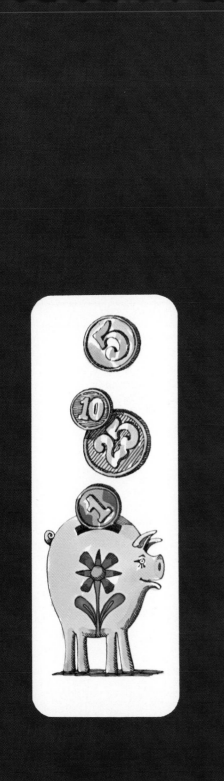

After you get money,
what can you buy?
When you spend money,
where does it go?
Why are hard-to-get things expensive?
How do you choose between two things?
Who pays for sidewalks and highways?

These questions are a part of
what grown-ups call economics.

On the next few pages, you will find
answers to many money questions
and you will learn
about some economic decisions
that you might have to make.

Decisions, decisions

Henry has enough money
to buy either a baseball and a bat
or a new pair of shoes.
Which will he choose?

If it's winter, he could buy
the shoes that he needs.
And maybe he could save enough, by the summer,
to buy the ball and bat.

If it's summer, Henry might decide
to buy the ball and bat
and wear his old shoes,
until he can save more money for new shoes.
To him, a summer of playing baseball
might be more important than having new shoes.

But if Henry just can't
go another week without new shoes,
he may have to give up his ball and bat
to buy the new shoes.
Sometimes, people have to give up what they want
to get what they need.

People have to make choices,
such as Henry's, all their lives.
Before they make a choice,
they usually compare the things they could choose.
Which costs more?
Which do they need now?
Which would they be better-off with in the long run?

MICHAEL MARTIN

Taking a chance

I climbed a tree to pick a ripe red apple.
The apple hung from the end of a thin branch.
I thought to myself—
    if I take a chance and climb out to get the apple,
    the branch will probably break.
    Then I'll fall and hurt myself.
    Is that apple worth so much that I should take
    the chance of hurting myself?
    It might be, if I were starving. But I'm not.
    That settles it.
Hurting myself wasn't worth the chance,
so I climbed back down the tree.

Whenever people take a chance, they have to guess
what might happen if they win,
and what might happen if they lose.
Then they can decide whether or not to take the chance.

A toymaker might make a new toy.
He knows that if people like it enough to buy it,
he will make money.
But if people don't like it enough to buy it,
he might lose the money he spent making the new toy.
If he thinks that people will probably buy the toy,
he might take the chance of making it.
If he thinks that people probably won't buy it,
he won't take the chance.

People take chances all the time.
Sometimes they win. Sometimes they lose.
That's the chance they take.

Where your dime goes

Suppose you pay a dime to a candy-shop owner
for a chocolate candy bar.

How much of that dime
can the shop owner keep for himself?
Probably, he can't keep any more
than two cents of the dime.
Even then, the government takes
part of the two cents for tax.

Where does the rest of the dime go?
The shop owner uses some of it
to pay for heat, electricity, water,
and other things he needs in the candy shop.

A little bit goes to the factory that made the candy bar.
And a little bit goes to the people
who ship the bar from the factory to the candy store.
Another little bit of the dime might pay
for a television commercial that advertises the bar.
Another bit pays for the chocolate, vanilla, sugar,
milk, nuts, and other things that go into the bar.
Still another bit goes to workers in other countries
who pick the sugar cane, vanilla plants, and cacao beans
(cacao is what chocolate is made from).
And another bit of the dime goes to the people
who work on the ships or planes that bring
the beans, vanilla, and sugar to this country.

Those are just some of the things
that happen to the dime you spent
for a chocolate candy bar.

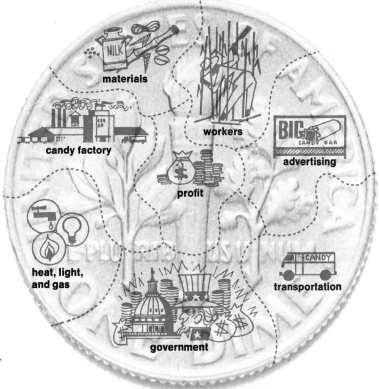

Candy-shop owners
spend money
in different ways.
Here are some
of the most important
places where
a shop owner's money
might go.

Breaking up a job into parts

You have just a few minutes to make ten peanut butter and jelly sandwiches for a picnic. You take out two pieces of bread, spread butter, peanut butter, and jelly on one piece. Then you cover it with the other piece of bread. That makes one sandwich. To make ten sandwiches, you have to do that nine more times. But you can make the sandwiches much faster if you break up the job into parts. Here's how it works.

First part: Take out ten pieces of bread and place them across a table.
Second part: Spread each piece with butter.
Third part: Spread each piece with peanut butter.
Fourth part: Spread each piece with jelly.
Fifth part: Take out ten more pieces of bread and cover each piece of bread across the table.

Give four of your friends a part of the job to do. Take a part for yourself, too.

| laying out the bread | spreading the butter | spreading the peanut butter | spreading the jelly | putting the bread together |

You could say that the sandwiches were made by a five-man assembly line. *To assemble* means "to put together." An assembly line is a group of people or machines that work together to make something. Each person or machine does one small part of a big job. Most factories use assembly lines. In an automobile factory, for example, each worker in an assembly line, with the help of machines, adds different parts to an automobile until it is built.

Sandwiches, automobiles, and almost everything else can be made more quickly when people use assembly lines.

automobile assembly line

333

television assembly line

Hard to get

Suppose you want to sell
your bicycle for ten dollars,
but no one will buy it.
You lower the price to eight dollars,
and still no one is interested.
The reason may be that
no one wants to buy a used bike.
Maybe people would rather buy a new one.

But let's suppose that suddenly,
all the bicycle factories closed,
and no one could buy new bicycles.
Then, maybe some people would want
to buy your old bike.

Your bike would be in demand.
You could probably sell it for more than
the ten dollars you first tried to sell it for.
And if you waited for a year or two,
so many people probably would want bicycles
that there wouldn't be enough bicycles for all of them.
Then, maybe you could sell your bicycle for fifty dollars.
And if you waited ten years,
you might get even more for it.
Some things—such as diamonds and natural pearls—
are expensive because there are very few of them,
and because many people want them.
And some things—such as paintings by famous artists—
are expensive because they are the only ones of their kind.

Money to
run a country

ICE CREAM SODA—65¢
If you buy that soda
in many places in the United States,
you have to pay 67¢.

Those extra pennies are a tax.
Tax is the word we use for money
that people have to give to a government
so that the government can pay
the expenses of running a country.

People pay taxes on
the food they eat,
the clothes they wear,
the light bulbs they see by,
the cars they travel in,
the houses they live in,
the medicine that helps them get well,
the money they make on a job,
and many other things.

Taxes pay for mailmen, policemen, and teachers—
for soldiers, pilots, and astronauts—
for jet fighters, space capsules,
post offices, and schools—
and for all the things the government buys.

Taxes that people pay help to pay
for many things that you use every day.
For example, the extra pennies you paid
for the ice cream soda
might have helped pay
for the sidewalks you walk on.

337

It pays
to advertise

What would television be like without commercials?
No interruptions of your favorite programs, for one thing.

But without commercials,
you probably wouldn't even be able
to watch a favorite TV program,
because, almost always, commercials pay for a program.

People who pay for commercials are called sponsors.
A sponsor might be a company that makes soap.
The sponsor might pay thousands of dollars
for a commercial to sell its soap.

The money the sponsor spends on a commercial
pays for actors, actresses, musicians, cameramen, lighting,
other workers in a television studio,
and everything else that goes into
arranging a program that you watch.

The sponsor gets money back
if people buy the soap that it advertises.

Newspapers and magazines have advertisements, too.
The advertisements help pay the people
who write and print the newspapers and magazines.
Advertisements even help pay
for your favorite comic strip.

How money can grow

If you fill a piggy bank
with ten dollars' worth of coins,
and keep it there for a year,
you still have just ten dollars
at the end of the year.

But if you put the ten dollars
in a savings account at a bank
and leave it there for a year,
the bank will add a little bit more money
to your ten dollars.
That extra money is called interest,
and the bank pays it to you.
The longer you leave your ten dollars
in the bank, the more interest you get.

Which would you rather have?

This?

Or this?

But where does a bank get the money
to pay you interest on your money?
They get it from other people
who borrow your money from the bank.
Let's say a friend of yours borrows
your ten dollars from the bank.
When he pays the money back to the bank,
he has to pay back the ten dollars—
and he has to pay some interest to the bank.
That's the price he pays for borrowing the money.
But he pays more interest to the bank
than the bank pays you on your money.
The bank keeps some of the interest
and pays some of it to you
for letting them use your money.

Ship out, ship in

Once upon a time, there was an island

in the middle of an ocean.

It was called Apple Island,

because the only fruit that grew

on the island was apples.

The people of Apple Island liked apples.

But after years and years of apple juice,

apples, apple cobblers, more apples, apple pies,

and still more apples, they did sometimes

wish they could taste something else.

One day, the King of Apple Island

decided to surprise his people.

He would get some lemons for them.

He would get the lemons from a nearby island

—an island called Lemon Island where only lemons grew.

He was almost sure that the people of Lemon Island

would be as glad to trade lemons for apples

as he was to trade apples for lemons.

And he was right.

Both islands

agreed to trade.

So the people of Apple Island started to *export*,

or ship out, their apples to Lemon Island

and *import*, or ship in, Lemon Island's lemons

to Apple Island.

Countries all over the world export and import things. When countries need or want something they don't have, they can import it from another country. In exchange, they can pay for the imports or they can export things that they have.

By exporting and importing things, people all over the world can enjoy and share things from many countries.

Start Your Own Town

How do we get towns?
How do people decide what they need?
Why don't you start your own town
and see?

Let's make you the mayor
of a make-believe town.
This week, you can pick
only 6 out of 18 buildings
that people want to build
in your town.
You must choose
what the people need most.

Turn the page, Mayor,
and start deciding.

Greeting cards,
gloves,
or groceries?

There they are, Mr. Mayor—
waiting for you at your office on Monday morning.
Mrs. Gripple wants to build a greeting card shop.
Mr. Grapple wants to build a glove store.
Mr. Gropple wants to build a grocery and meat market.
Gripple?
Grapple?
Gropple?
Whose place will give the people of your town
what they need most?
Will you decide on
—a place where people can buy greeting cards?
—a place where people can buy gloves?
—or a place where people can buy groceries and meat?

Cameras,
clothes,
or camellias?

Now it's Tuesday, Mr. Mayor,
and three more people are standing in line
outside your office
wanting building permits.

Mr. Cling wants to build a camera store.
Mr. Clang wants to build a clothing store.
And Mrs. Clong wants to build a camellia shop.
What do the people of your town need the most
—a place where they can buy cameras?
—a place where they can buy clothes for the family?
—or a place where they can buy flowers?

As the mayor,
what do you decide?

Classrooms, clocks, or candy?

On Wednesday morning, Mr. Mayor,
you get three telephone calls.

Mr. Care wants to build some classrooms.
Mr. Core wants to build a clock store.
Mr. Cure wants to build a candy shop.
Which place will fill a need
for the most people in your town
—classrooms for a school
where children can get an education?
—a clock store where people can get clocks?
—or a candy shop
where people can get candy?

Well, Mr. Mayor,
which man gets the building permit—
Mr. Care, Mr. Core, or Mr. Cure?

Harness,
hardware,
or health?

Three more people are waiting for you
when you get to your office on Thursday, Mr. Mayor.
Mr. Hale wants to build a harness shop.
Mr. Hare wants to build a hardware store.
Mr. Hill wants to build a health clinic
with offices for doctors and dentists.

Which do the people of your town need most
—a place where they can go to doctors and dentists?
—a place where they can get harnesses?
—or a place where they can get things made from metal?
Make up your mind, Mr. Mayor.
Which building gets built?

Drugstore,
dime store,
or doughnuts?

Friday morning, Mr. Mayor,
three more people are sitting in your office
waiting for you to decide
which one gets a building permit.
Mr. Diddle wants to build a drugstore.
Mr. Daddle wants to build a dime store.
Mrs. Duddle wants to build a doughnut shop.
Now you must decide which store
the people in your town need most
—a store where they can get
their doctors' prescriptions filled?
—a store where they can buy some things for a dime?
—or a store where they can buy doughnuts?
You're the mayor.
You decide.

A bank,
a barbershop,
or a button store?

Here it is Saturday, Mr. Mayor,
and you're in your office again.
Three more people are waiting to learn
which one you'll give a building permit to.

Mr. Blimey wants to build a bank.
Mr. Bloomey wants to build a barbershop.
Mr. Blay wants to build a button store.

Which do the people in your town need most
—a bank where they can save and borrow money?
—a barbershop where men and boys
can get haircuts?
—or a button store where women can buy buttons?

Your office closes at noon, Mr. Mayor,
so you'd better make up your mind fast.
To see if you made wise decisions, turn the page.

The mayor's choice

You deserve to be the mayor of your town
if you have chosen the places shown on these pages,
because these places fill a need
for just about everybody who lives in your town.
But don't feel bad if you made different choices.
After all, you're the mayor—
and you know what your town needs.

Changing Things; Saving Things

Take trees.
Many people have.
They have cut down too many,
too fast.
Without trees, the soil is washed
away very rapidly.

Take coal.
Many people have.
They have stripped large amounts
of land, harming the soil
and making whole areas ugly.

Take water.
Many people have.
They have made it dirty—
unfit for you to swim in
or fish to live in.

Some things must be saved
or they will be gone forever.
Others can be changed and used again.

What is being done? Can you help?
Read the next few pages and find out.

361

A useless mountain of
metal junk ruins the
scenery nearby.

An old car is picked up
by an overhead crane.
The car will be broken
into small pieces and
then shipped to a steel
factory for remelting.

Can cans and cars
be cans and cars again?

Play this game! As you walk or ride to school, count all the throwaway cans you see along the way. Can you do it or are there too many?

Used cans, old cars, and other metal things can make parks, country roads, and city streets look like garbage dumps. That's why it's important to gather them up. This used metal is called scrap metal. Scrap metal can be used again—it can be recycled.

Cans and other metal scraps can be collected and sold back to an aluminum or steel factory. There, machines press thousands of cans and other scrap metal into squares the size of trucks. The squares are melted and made into new cans or other things.

And cars? A car-gobbling machine mashes a useless car into fist-sized chunks in a minute. New steel is melted with the old steel to produce new cars.

Saving newspapers and taking them to a collection center helps save trees.

Growing up green

A world without trees? What would you climb up, sit under, or hide behind? Where would you build your tree fort? Where would you tie your tent?

Trees are important. They shade us and often feed us. Trees house animals and feed them, too. Trees keep the soil from washing away when it rains. Besides being so helpful, trees add beauty everywhere.

Trees give us many things. Paper is one of the most important products from trees. To make paper, we have to cut down trees. Then how can we have both paper and trees? One way is to make new paper from old paper. How? You can help.

First, save old newspapers and magazines. Then give the old paper to someone who will take it to a paper mill. At the mill, special machines beat the old paper into a mushy pulp. They clean the pulp of all metal, ink, and dirt. Then the pulp goes into a paper machine and comes out as clean, new paper. All this without cutting down one climbing, hiding, shading tree.

A fork truck moves a bundle of wastepaper in a paper plant. The old paper will be cleaned and made into new paper.

See-through sand

Have you ever tasted sandy soda, grainy pickles, or gritty applesauce? Probably not. Even though many foods come in containers made from sand, they don't taste sandy. What kind of container? Glass. Glass is made of sand. It can be filled with food, looked through, cooled, warmed, and used over and over.

There is plenty of sand in the world, so why use glass more than once? To save energy. Making glass from sand takes more energy than making it from old glass. Another reason is less litter. Re-used glass does not become roadside trash.

Bottles that can be filled again are called returnables. They can be used several times before being made into new bottles.

Throwaway bottles cannot be refilled. But they can be collected, sent to a factory, and made into new bottles.

Urge your parents to buy bottled drinks in returnable bottles. If they aren't returnable, take them to a collection center instead of a trash can. The barrels of sorted glass will be sent to a factory to be made into new glass.

Soda pop often comes in returnable bottles. These bottles can be refilled and used again and again.

Glass jars and bottles are brought to collection centers. From there, they are taken to a glass factory where the bottles and jars are smashed, melted, and made into new glass containers.

Drip, drip, drip

Listen to the water—drip, drip, drip—a leaky faucet.
Listen to the water—whoosh, gurgle, gurgle—a draining bath.
Listen to the water—whish, whish, whish—a running sprinkler.

Listen to the sounds of water being wasted—drip, gurgle, whish.
We shouldn't waste water. Without it, we could not live.

Some places have plenty of water. Some places are very dry.
But almost any city or town can run short of water. This happens if people use too much or if it doesn't rain for a long time.

People are often careless with their water, too. Sometimes they waste it or pollute it. If your city or town runs short of water, it's important that everyone becomes a water watcher.

How can you help when the water is low?
1) Use water wisely. Take a shower instead of a bath. A shower takes half as much water as a bath.
2) Turn the faucets on only when you need water. Don't let a faucet run while brushing your teeth or waiting for the water to get cold. Cold water can be kept in the refrigerator.
3) Save cooking water. After it cools, use it to water house and garden plants.
4) Be sure that your house has no drippy, leaky faucets.
5) Catch rain water in a plastic trash can. It's great for watering outdoor gardens and indoor plants.
6) Your family can save water by leaving cars unwashed and lawns unsprinkled.

Breaking open fire
hydrants wastes water.

Fixing a leaky faucet is a job for the whole family.
All those drips add up to a lot of wasted water.

Breathe in (cough)

It stings your eyes. It tickles your nose. It scratches your throat. It can even make you sick.

What is it? It's air pollution. Polluted air is dirty, dangerous air. It often smells bad. It often looks bad. And it often harms and sometimes kills living things.

How does air get dirty? Burning causes most pollution. Cars burn gasoline. Factories burn coal. And dumps burn garbage. More cars, factories, and dumps mean more filthy air.

Some polluted air is called smog. Smog is *sm*oke mixed with f*og*. Foggy cities everywhere often have smoggy skies.

What is being done to clean the air? Cars have devices to cut down gasoline fumes. Factories switch from coal to cleaner fuels. And tons of garbage are being reused instead of being burned.

Fresh air for sale! A Tokyo girl buys a few breaths of oxygen.

This machine measures a car's exhaust fumes. If the fumes are too great, the car must be fixed. Testing centers (*below*) are set up in places around the city.

A little litter

Throw your pop can out the car window.
It's easy.
Toss your candy wrapper on the ground.
It's easy.
Dump your picnic trash on the beach.
It's easy.

It's easy to litter.
And it's even easier to see why litter
makes things ugly and unsafe.
Littered areas look horrible.
And they attract germs and animals that carry germs.

If you like green grass, sandy beaches, and clean streets,
help keep them that way.
Walk to the nearest trash container and drop your trash there—
it's easy.

Beaches and carnivals draw crowds of people.
Crowds always have lots to eat and drink. And
this means litter. Do you help clean up like
the boys on the beach or do you litter like
many carnival-goers?

Mash, bury, and spray

Scruuunch! A machine mashes mountains of trash
into small squares of scrap metal.
Plunk! Crash! Bang! The squares of scrap metal
are bulldozed into a huge ditch and covered with dirt.
After the ditch is shaped into a hill,
a skiing-sledding slope is built.

Swish! Swish! Swish! A giant, squirt-gun machine
sprays acres of land with a city's waste water.
Large power shovels have ripped and stripped the land
for its coal. The soil needs to be nourished before
crops can be planted again. And the sprayed-on water enriches
the soil. One day, the food grown on this useless land
will feed many people living in the city.

Wasting wastes is wasteful. Garbage, trash, and sewage
do not have to be dumped or burned.
They can be scrunched, plunked, and swished.

Sprayed-on waste water helps plants to grow.

Mount Trashmore in Illinois was built from layers of garbage covered by dirt. The hill is used for skiing and sledding.

Save your energy

Freeze it. Cook it. Cool it.
Wash it. Dry it. Iron it.
Plug it in. Turn it on. Turn it up.

Just about everything in your house needs electricity to work. Look around. What do you see? A television, a lamp, an air conditioner, a refrigerator, a toaster—all powered by electricity.

Electricity is not free. People buy it. Electricity is made by burning coal or other fuel to make steam. The steam powers big machines that make electricity. If the fuel runs out, so does the electricity. With more and more people using more and more electricity, this could happen.

On some days, the lights may brown out or dim. On some days, the TV's picture may shrink. Why? Because too many people are using too much electricity. Give your house an electric checkup and save your energy.

Big-city blackouts, like this one, can be caused by using too much electric power. Only the glimmer of a few emergency lights breaks the darkness.

Do you turn off your lights
when they are not needed?

Do you shut the refrigerator
door tightly?

Do you turn off the TV before
going outside?

Do you turn down the air conditioner
when leaving the room for a long time?

Illustration Acknowledgments

The publishers of *Childcraft* gratefully acknowledge the following artists, photographers, publishers, agencies, and corporations for illustrations in this volume. Page numbers refer to two-page spreads. The words "*(left)*," "*(center)*," "*(top)*," "*(bottom)*," and "*(right)*," indicate position on the spread. All illustrations are the exclusive property of the publishers of *Childcraft* unless names are marked with an asterisk (*).

1: Robert Keys
4-5: John Alcorn
6-7: *(top)* Martin-Trlak Inc.; *(bottom, left to right)* Madagascar Vanilla Growers *, Field Museum of Natural History Chicago *, Arthur H. Fisher *, Charles Perry Weimer *
8-9: H. P. Hood and Sons, Inc. *
10-11: art, Paul McNear; photo, National Biscuit Company *
12-13: *(left)* Rainey Bennett; *(right)* Affy Tapple, Inc. *
14-15: photo, Pepsi-Cola Company *; art, Paul McNear
16-17: *(left)* Knox Gelatin Inc., Johnstown, N.Y. *; *(right)* art, Robert Lawson, photo, Don Stebbing
18-19: art, Charles Harper; photos, National Film Board of Canada *
20-21: *(left)* Robert Keys *(right)* Switzerland Cheese Association, Inc. *
22-23: *(left)* Interstate Brands Corporation *; *(right)* John M. Bolt, Jr.
24-25: *(left)* Arthur Rickerby *Life* © Time Inc. *; *(right)* Pat Rosado
26-27: *(left)* Alan Band Associates *; *(right)* The Buhler Corporation *
28-29: art, John Hollis; photos, *(left)* Don Stebbing, *(right)* Kellogg Company *
30-31: *(left)* Hollis Alling; *(right)* photo, Rie Gaddis Wehrmann, art, Pat Rosado
32-33: *(left)* photo, Charles Perry Weimer *, art, Paul McNear; *(right)* William Wrigley, Jr. Company *
34-35: art, James Teason; photo, J. I. Case Co. *
36-37: *(left)* *Childcraft* photo by Jim Collins; *(right)* Tom Goleas
38-39: *(left)* Don Stebbing; *(right)* Jay Foods, Inc. *
40-41: *(left)* Darrow M. Watt *; *(right: top to bottom)* Chicken of the Sea Brand Tuna *, Japan Tourist Association *, Devaney *
42-43: Grant Heilman *
44-45: *(left)* Ted Carr; *(right)* Bowman Dairy Company *
46-47: Neal Cochran
48-49: *(left)* Rie Gaddis Wehrmann, General Mills, Inc. *; *(right)* *Childcraft* photo
50-51: Raymond Perlman
52-53: Bill Rhodes
54-55: *(left)* Monsanto Chemical Co. *; *(right: top to bottom)* 1 and 2, United Press Int. *; 3, Art Rogers, *Los Angeles Times* *; 4, Wide World *
56-57: *(left)* Carl Frank, Photo Researchers *; *(top right)* Tom Goleas; *(bottom right)* Mart Studio
58-59: Jack Smith
60-61: *(left)* *Welding Engineer Magazine* *; *(top and center right)* *Childcraft* photos; *(bottom right)* Alfa Studio and United States Steel Corp. *
62-63: James Teason
64-65: Robert Kresin
66-67: Neal Cochran
68-69: *(left)* NASA *; *(right)* George Roth
70-71: Minnesota Mining & Manufacturing Co. *
72-73: Jim Joseph
74-75: art, Roy Andersen; photos, *(left)* Wide World *, *(right)* United Press Int. *

76-77: *(top left)* U.S. Navy *; *(top right)* Kolbrener-Portnoy Photography *; *(bottom left)* International *Harvester Today* *; *(bottom right)* Donald McKellar
78-79: *(left)* photos, Chicago Fire Department *, United Press Int. *, art, Robert Christiansen; *(right)* Quantas Airways *
80-81: Dean Wessel
82-83: James Teason
84-85: *(bottom left)* *Childcraft*, courtesy U.S. Army; *(top)* *Childcraft* photos; *(bottom right)* Karsh, Rapho Guillumette *
86-87: *(left)* Jim Joseph; *(right)* Alfa Studio
88-89: art, Ross Rohrer; photos, Clyde Akin *
90-91: George Roth
92-93: John Alcorn
94-95: art, Peter Steenveld; photos, Colgate-Palmolive Company *
96-97: *(left)* art, Paul McNear, photos, E. I. du Pont de Nemours & Company *; *(right)* Don Stebbing
98-99: *(left)* Clayton Peterson, *The Salinas Californian* *; *(right)* Don Stebbing
100-101: *(left)* Clark Bruorton; *(top right)* National-Standard Company *; *(bottom right)* Vince Hill Studio
102-103: *(left)* Peter Steenveld; *(top right)* International Harvester Company *; *(bottom right)* Coats & Clark, Inc. *
104-105: art, Luke Doheny; photos, Wilson Sporting Goods Company*
106-107: *(left)* Art Seiden; *(right)* Don Stebbing
108-109: *(left)* Don Stebbing; *(right)* Martha Roberts *
110-111: art, William J. Bryan; photos, Kingsport Press, Inc.
112-113: Martin J. Schmidt *
114-115: *(top)* Skutt & Sons *; *(bottom)* Syracuse China Corporation *
116-117: *(left)* Wilson Sporting Goods Company *; *(right)* John M. Bolt, Jr.
118-119: *(left)* Flambeau Plastics Corp. *; *(center)* Strombeck Manufacturing Co. *; *(right)* *Chicago Sun-Times* *
120-121: *(left)* Don Stebbing; *(right)* The Florsheim Shoe Company *
122-123: photos, Firestone News Service, Akron *; art, Paul McNear
124-125: *(left)* Eastman Chemical Products, Inc. *; *(top right)* Constance Brown, Eldon Industries, Inc. *; *(bottom right)* *Childcraft* photo, courtesy Mattel, Inc.
126-127: *(left)* Sunbeam Corporation *; *(right)* B. Kuppenheimer & Co., Inc. *
128-129: United Piece Dye Works *
130-131: *(left)* Eastfoto *; *(top right)* American Stock photo from Bruce Coleman, Inc. *, *(bottom right)* Orion Press *
132-133: *(left)* Don Taka; *(right)* Don Stebbing
134-135: *(left)* and *top right)* N.W. Ayer & Son, Inc. *; *(bottom right)* Tiffany and Company *
136-137: photos, Diamond National Corporation *; art, Paul McNear
138-139: *(left)* Paul McNear; *(top right)* American Smelting and Refining Company *; *(bottom right)* George Burns, *Saturday Evening Post*, © Curtis Publishing Company *
140-141: *(left)* Corning Glass Works *; *(right)* Owens-Illinois *
142-143: *(top)* Owens-Illinois *; *(bottom right)* Frank Fenner *
144-145: Corning Glass Center *
146-147: Tom Goleas
148-149: *(left)* Carl Yates; *(right)* Structural Clay Products Institute *
150-151: American Forest Institute *
152-153: *(left)* Rutherford Platt *; *(right)* Diamond National Corporation *
154-155: *(left)* Paul McNear; photos, *(top right)* Caterpillar Tractor Company *, *(bottom right)* American Forest Products Industries *
156-157: Don Stebbing
158-159: PPG Industries *
160-161: Carl Koch
162-163: *(top left)* Corning Glass Works *; *(bottom left)* Don Stebbing; *(right)* Paul McNear
164-165: art, Paul McNear; photos, Standard Oil Company of California *

166-167: Raymond Perlman and John Alcorn
168-169: Dorothy McLaughlin
170-171: art, Pat Doyle; photo, Rie Gaddis Wehrmann
172-173: Dean Wessel
174-175: Tom Goleas
176-177: Francis Chase
178-179: Tom Goleas
180-181: Robert Kresin
182-183: (left) Childcraft photo by Tom Stack; (right) Henry Monroe, DPI *
184-185: (left) Joe Molnar *; (top right) James Annan *, (center and bottom right) Rie Gaddis Wehrmann *
186-187: (top left) Childcraft photo; (bottom left) Rie Gaddis Wehrmann *; (right) Childcraft photo
188-189: (left) Childcraft photo; (right) Childcraft photos by Chester Sheard
190-191: Childcraft photos
192-193: Mary Miller Salem
194-195: (left and right top and center) Rie Gaddis Wehrmann; (bottom right) Childcraft photo
196-197: (left and bottom right) Rie Gaddis Wehrmann *; (top right) Jim Collins
198-199: (left) Don Loehle; (right) Rie Gaddis Wehrmann *
200-201: (left) Jim Joseph; (right) Rie Gaddis Wehrmann *
202-203: (top left) Bea Rosenthal, Photofind *; (top right) Marjorie Pickens; (bottom left, left to right) Jim Collins, Ilka Hartmann, Jeroboam, Inc. *; (bottom right) Grete Mannheim, DPI *
204-205: (left) Childcraft photos by Jim Collins; (top right) Childcraft photo; (bottom right) Ebony magazine *
206-207: (left) Department of Public Works of Chicago *; (right) Chicago Dept. of Water and Sewers *
208-209: (left) Richard Loehle; (top right) Health Dept., City of Chicago *; (bottom right) Childcraft photo
210-211: (left) John M. Bolt, Jr.; (right) Childcraft photos
212-213: Caterpillar Tractor Company *
214-215: (top left) Enjay Chemical Co., a division of Humble Oil & Refining Co. *, (bottom left) Bureau of Sanitation, City of Chicago *; (right) Paul McNear
216-217: art, Richard Loehle; photo, Sewage Commission, City of Milwaukee *
218-219: (left) John M. Bolt, Jr.; (right) National Weather Service *
220-221: John Alcorn and Raymond Perlman
222-223: (left) United Press Int. *; (right) James H. Brown
224-225: art, Jan Balet *; photos, Weldon-Roberts Rubber Company *
226-227: The Parker Pen Company *; (bottom right) Don Stebbing
228-229: art, Mary Horton; photos, (top) Charles Gekler, Chicago Sun-Times *, (center) International Paper Company *, (bottom, left to right) Charles Gekler, Chicago Sun-Times *, International Paper Company *, William Vandivert *
230-231: (left) Childcraft photo; (right) The American Crayon Company *
232-233: (left) Weber Costello Company *; (right) Peter Steenveld
234-235: (left) The American Crayon Company *; (right) Paul McNear
236-237: Don Loehle
238-239: U.S. Postal Service *
240-241: (right) Orlando, Three Lions *
242-243: (left) United Press Int. *, art, Don Loehle; (right) Frank Fenner
244-247: Kong Wu
248-249: WGN Continental Broadcasting Company *
250-251: art, Paul McNear; photos, (left) MOTOROLA *, (top right) Chicago Fire Department *, (bottom left) General Electric *
252-253: (left) Tom Morgan; (top right) United Press Int. *, (bottom right) King Radio Corp. *
254-255: (left) Franklin McMahon; (top right) Childcraft photo; (bottom right) Frank Fenner
256-257: (left) Franklin McMahon; (top right) Childcraft photo, (center right) WGN-Channel 9, Chicago, * and Childcraft photos; (bottom right) E. F. Hoppe
258-259: (left) Franklin McMahon; (right) Ralph Walters, Chicago Sun-Times *
260-261: (right) Franklin McMahon; (left) Chicago Sun-Times *
262-263: (left) Childcraft photo; (right) International Business Machines Corp. *
264-265: John Alcorn and Raymond Perlman
266-267: John M. Bolt, Jr.
268-269: George Roth
270-271: (top left to bottom right) 1 and 5, Santa Fe Railway *; 2, 3, and 4, Association of American Railroads *
272-273: art, Bill Hammond; photos, (left) Mart Studio, (right) Santa Fe Railway *
274-275: (top) Reading Company *; (bottom) William Vandivert *
276-277: Carl Koch
278-279: Raymond Perlman
280-281: (left, bottom right) United States Lines *; (top right) U.S. Coast Guard *
282-283: (left) French Line *; (top right) Cunard Line *; (bottom right) Stanley Rosenthall, DeWys, Inc. *
284-285: Mary Hauge
286-287: (top) Dmitri Kessel, Life © Time Inc. *; (bottom left) United Airlines *; (bottom right) Childcraft photo
288-289: United Airlines *
290-291: (top) Department of Transport, Ottawa *; (bottom left) United Air Lines *; (bottom right) Metro News Photos *
292-293: art, Tom Morgan; photos, United Air Lines *
294-295: United Air Lines *
296-297: Childcraft photos
298-299: Vernon McKissack
300-301: (left) Ed Simonek; (right) Continental Trailways *
302-303: John Alcorn
304-305: art, Robert Kresin; photos (balboa, peso, rupee) Krause Publications *, Childcraft photos; (sol) Don Stebbing; (yen) Childcraft photo; all others courtesy Chase Manhattan Bank Money Museum *
306-307: (left) Boris Artzybasheff; (center right) Chase Manhattan Bank Money Museum *, all others, Buffalo Museum of Science *
308-309: William J. Bryan
310-311: (left) Don Stebbing; (right) Carl Yates
312-313: (left) Don Stebbing; (center and right) Three Lions *
314-315: Don Stebbing
316-317: (left) U.S. Bureau of Engraving and Printing *; (right) Bankers Trust Company, New York *
318-319: (left, top to bottom) Jewel Companies, Inc. *, Monroe International Calculating *; (right, top to bottom) National Cash Register Co.*, Brandt Automatic Cashier Co. *
320-321: (left) Jo Anna Poehlmann; (right) Don Stebbing
322-323: First Federal Savings and Loan Association of Chicago *
324-325: John Alcorn
326-327: Michael Martin
328-329: George Suyeoka
330-331: (left) Childcraft photo; (right) John M. Bolt, Jr.
332-333: art, Gene Sharp; photos, (top) Childcraft photo, (center) Ford Motor Company *, (bottom) Radio Corporation of America *
334-337: Gene Sharp
338-339: Suzi Hawes
340-341: John M. Bolt, Jr.
342-343: Suzi Hawes
344-345: John Alcorn
346-359: Gene Sharp
360-361: John Alcorn and Raymond Perlman
362-363: (left) Don Stebbing; (right) World Book photo
364-365: (top) Childcraft photo by Jim Collins; (bottom) World Book photo
366-367: (left) Childcraft photo by Jim Collins; (right) World Book photos
368-369: (left) Mark Kane from Katherine Young *; (right) Vernon McKissack
370-371: (left) Orion Press *; (right) Childcraft photos *
372-373: (left) Vernon McKissack; (right) Phoebe Dunn, DPI *
374-375: (left) Childcraft photo *; (right) Metropolitan Sanitary District of Greater Chicago *
376-377: (left) Arthur Rickerby, Life © Time Inc. *; (right) Vernon McKissack

Heritage binding cover—(left to right): (back) Tom Coleas, Childcraft photo, Bill Rhodes, Childcraft photo; (spine) Childcraft photo; (front) Carl Koch, Childcraft photo, John Alcorn, Childcraft photo

Index

This index is an alphabetical list of the important topics covered in this book. It will help you find information given in both words *and* pictures. To help you understand what an entry means, there is often a helping word in parentheses. For example, **latex** (tree product). If there is information in both words and pictures, you will see the words *with pictures* after the page number. If there is *only* a picture, you will see the word *picture* before the page number. If you do not find what you want in this index, please go to the General Index in Volume 15, which is a key to all of the books.